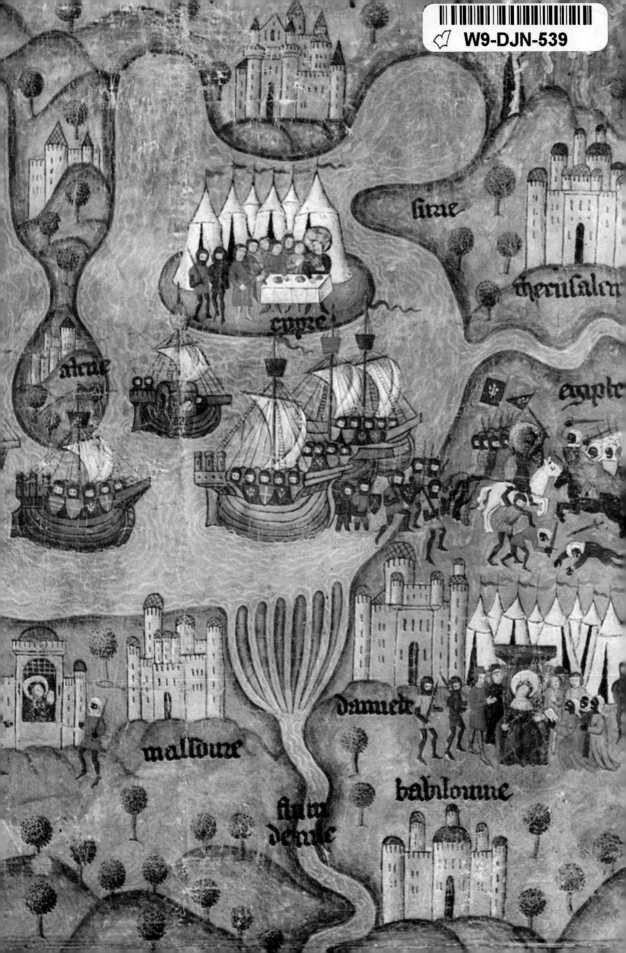

W9-DJN-539

There are a number of HORIZON CARAVEL BOOKS published each year. Titles now available are:

BEETHOVEN
THE SEARCH FOR KING ARTHUR
CONSTANTINOPLE, CITY ON THE GOLDEN HORN
LORENZO DE' MEDICI AND THE RENAISSANCE
MASTER BUILDERS OF THE MIDDLE AGES
PIZARRO AND THE CONQUEST OF PERU
FERDINAND AND ISABELLA
CHARLEMAGNE
CHARLES DARWIN AND THE ORIGIN OF SPECIES
RUSSIA IN REVOLUTION
DESERT WAR IN NORTH AFRICA
THE BATTLE OF WATERLOO
THE HOLY LAND IN THE TIME OF JESUS
THE SPANISH ARMADA
BUILDING THE SUEZ CANAL
MOUNTAIN CONQUEST
PHARAOHS OF EGYPT
LEONARDO DA VINCI
THE FRENCH REVOLUTION
CORTES AND THE AZTEC CONQUEST
CAESAR
THE UNIVERSE OF GALILEO AND NEWTON
THE VIKINGS
MARCO POLO'S ADVENTURES IN CHINA
SHAKESPEARE'S ENGLAND
CAPTAIN COOK AND THE SOUTH PACIFIC
THE SEARCH FOR EARLY MAN
JOAN OF ARC
EXPLORATION OF AFRICA
NELSON AND THE AGE OF FIGHTING SAIL
ALEXANDER THE GREAT
RUSSIA UNDER THE CZARS
HEROES OF POLAR EXPLORATION
KNIGHTS OF THE CRUSADES

American Heritage also publishes AMERICAN HERITAGE JUNIOR LIBRARY books, a similar series on American history. Titles now available are:

FRANKLIN DELANO ROOSEVELT
LABOR ON THE MARCH, THE STORY OF AMERICA'S UNIONS
THE BATTLE OF THE BULGE
THE BATTLE OF YORKTOWN
THE HISTORY OF THE ATOMIC BOMB
TO THE PACIFIC WITH LEWIS AND CLARK
THEODORE ROOSEVELT, THE STRENUOUS LIFE
GEORGE WASHINGTON AND THE MAKING OF A NATION
CAPTAINS OF INDUSTRY
CARRIER WAR IN THE PACIFIC
JAMESTOWN: FIRST ENGLISH COLONY
AMERICANS IN SPACE
ABRAHAM LINCOLN IN PEACE AND WAR
AIR WAR AGAINST HITLER'S GERMANY
IRONCLADS OF THE CIVIL WAR
THE ERIE CANAL
THE MANY WORLDS OF BENJAMIN FRANKLIN
COMMODORE PERRY IN JAPAN
THE BATTLE OF GETTYSBURG
ANDREW JACKSON, SOLDIER AND STATESMAN
ADVENTURES IN THE WILDERNESS
LEXINGTON, CONCORD AND BUNKER HILL
CLIPPER SHIPS AND CAPTAINS
D-DAY, THE INVASION OF EUROPE
WESTWARD ON THE OREGON TRAIL
THE FRENCH AND INDIAN WARS
GREAT DAYS OF THE CIRCUS
STEAMBOATS ON THE MISSISSIPPI
COWBOYS AND CATTLE COUNTRY
TEXAS AND THE WAR WITH MEXICO
THE PILGRIMS AND PLYMOUTH COLONY
THE CALIFORNIA GOLD RUSH
PIRATES OF THE SPANISH MAIN
TRAPPERS AND MOUNTAIN MEN
MEN OF SCIENCE AND INVENTION
NAVAL BATTLES AND HEROES
THOMAS JEFFERSON AND HIS WORLD
DISCOVERERS OF THE NEW WORLD
RAILROADS IN THE DAYS OF STEAM
INDIANS OF THE PLAINS
THE STORY OF YANKEE WHALING

COVER: *A squad of knights ride out to war in all the colorful trappings of the Middle Ages.*
ADAPTED FROM A MANUSCRIPT ILLUMINATION, THE PIERPONT MORGAN LIBRARY

FRONT END SHEET: *This map of the Mediterranean chronicles the Crusades of King Louis IX.*
THE METROPOLITAN MUSEUM OF ART

TITLE PAGE: *In a contemporary sketch Saladin is shown wresting the True Cross from Richard.*
CORPUS CHRISTI COLLEGE, CAMBRIDGE

BACK END SHEET: *Nearly all the weapons of siege warfare are painted into this colorful scene.*
BIBLIOTHEQUE NATIONALE

A HORIZON CARAVEL BOOK

KNIGHTS OF THE
CRUSADES

By the Editors of
HORIZON MAGAZINE

Author
JAY WILLIAMS

Consultant
MARGARET B. FREEMAN
Curator of The Cloisters, The Metropolitan Museum of Art, New York City

Published by American Heritage Publishing Co., Inc.
Book Trade and Institutional Distribution by
Harper & Row

FIFTH PRINTING

Library of Congress Catalogue Card Number: 62–11593
© 1962 by American Heritage Publishing Co., Inc., 551 Fifth Avenue, New York, New York, 10017. All rights reserved under Berne and Pan-American Copyright Conventions.
Trademark CARAVEL registered United States Patent Office

UNITY SCHOOL LIBRARY
UNITY VILLAGE, MISSOURI 64065

WITHDRAWN
by Unity Library

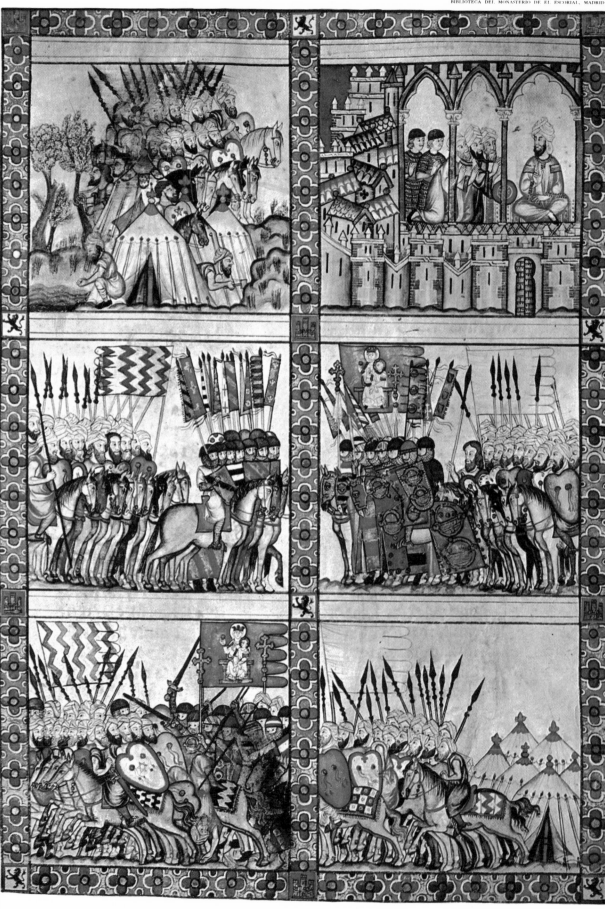

FOREWORD

However great their initial triumphs, the Crusades failed from a long-range military standpoint. Yet these tragic wars to recover the Holy Land from the infidel have left the world richer for memories of heroism and endurance, devotion and high adventure.

The period of the Crusades was also one of remarkable and lasting achievements in the field of the peaceful arts. During the centuries between 1095 when Pope Urban II preached the First Crusade and 1291 when the last Christian stronghold in the Holy Land fell to the Moslems, thousands of churches and cathedrals were being constructed and decorated throughout Europe. Modern man can scarcely comprehend the vast amount of manpower and money, the engineering ability, and the artistic skill expended in this phenomenal wave of building. Among the better-known monuments of this era are the magnificent Cathedral of Notre Dame in Paris and the exquisite little Sainte Chapelle, which King Louis IX built as a shrine for the sacred relics he brought back from the Holy Land. The noble Cathedral of Rheims and the unsurpassed Cathedral of Chartres, with its sculptures and brilliant stained-glass windows, were also built during these centuries.

The era of the Crusades, like the entire Middle Ages, is noteworthy too for the production of beautiful books. These manuscripts were written by hand, as the name implies, and illustrated sometimes naïvely and at other times with an expertness that a modern artist might well envy. They are not only prized treasures in themselves but are also colorful and lively sources of information for the history and customs of the times. Many illustrations from the manuscripts are reproduced in the pages of this book.

There was a time when the crusading age was portrayed as "dark" and of little cultural value. But it is now recognized, in both its failures and its triumphs, as one of the truly great periods in the history of mankind.

MARGARET B. FREEMAN

A battle painted as a comic strip: Moslems scout a Christian city (top); the Christians are surrounded (center); they fight their way clear (bottom).

BIBLIOTECA DEL MONASTERIO DE EL ESCORIAL, MADRID

There were frequent intervals of productive peace between the battles of the Crusades. Here a knight plays a peaceful game of chess with a Moslem companion.

CONTENTS

I CONQUEST!

PERMISSION OF THE TRUSTEES OF THE BRITISH MUSEUM

Duke William

The Crusades carried fire and sword from Europe under the banner of the Christian Church into the Biblical lands of the Middle East. The first of them occurred more than eight hundred years ago, when Europe was only beginning to recover from the disruption of the Dark Ages. At that time the Arab nations of the eastern Mediterranean were, by contrast, united and civilized.

Thirty years before the First Crusade, the Norman Conquest took place. That invasion of England in 1066 still gives the best available close-up picture of how the early crusading knights fought—and of some of the motives that made them ride into battle.

The thunderous encounter of October 14, 1066, has come to be called the Battle of Hastings. It was recorded, soon after the event, by an unknown English monk:

Then Duke William sailed from Normandy into Pevensy. When King Harold was informed of this, he gathered together a great host and came to oppose him at the grey apple tree, and William came upon him unexpectedly before his army was set in order. Nevertheless, the King fought against him most resolutely . . . and there was great slaughter on both sides. King Harold was slain, and Leofwine his brother and Earl Gyrth his brother, and many good men. The French had possession of the place of slaughter, as God granted them because of the nation's sins.

Thus came the Normans from France across the Channel to England, clinching their conquest of the country in one head-on engagement. But to understand how the battle was fought and what resulted from that day, it should be looked at in greater detail.

A bold band of French warriors stormed across the English Channel with William the Conqueror in 1066. With their superior armor and weapons and tighter discipline they were triumphant. Their swift conquest of England marked the end of the Viking era and the beginning of knightly warfare.

BIBLIOTHÈQUE NATIONALE, SERVICE PHOTOGRAPHIQUE

11

Harold Godwinson had been made king of the English early in January of 1066. He was not the son of the old king, for Edward the Confessor had died childless. But he was by all odds the most powerful of the several provincial rulers whose lands were together called England. There was not then the system of a strong central kingdom and of a crown passed down from son to son that was to characterize the nation in later ages. It was the king's function not to rule, but to fight, and to lead whatever troops he could find into battle.

At the time of Harold's coming to the throne the country was imperiled by two threats: the first was another wild and reckless raid from Scandinavia, where the Vikings and their restless heirs were still active; the second was an invasion from the French coast.

Across the Channel, Duke William of Normandy claimed the crown of England as his own. And if Harold was hailed as a great chieftain, Duke William was a leader of even greater stature. He was a worthy master of his ruthless and invincible warriors; a man who in twenty years had made his name the greatest on the European continent.

In the spring of 1066 Duke William began to make preparations for the invasion of England. He first won over those of his own followers who were lukewarm about the operation. He made his peace with the new king of France, Philip I, by promising that he would hold England as Philip's representative. And—a most important move— he got the support of Pope Alexander II, who agreed that William was the true heir of the English throne because of his wife's royal English blood. The Pope sent William a banner marked with a cross to signify that his cause, like so many other bloody adventures that would soon follow, was considered a holy crusade. And under that banner William gathered a mighty army in which were not only his own Normans but many French, Breton, Flemish, and Aquitanian knights who had joined him in the never-failing hope of winning wealth.

PHOTO BY J. COMBIER

The best contemporary record of the Norman Conquest is the Bayeux Tapestry. *A section of this early 12th-century embroidery (left) shows King Harold being warned by an appearance of Halley's comet that 1066 would be a fateful year. After overcoming the Norwegians at Stamford Bridge (see map, right), he hurried south with his weary men and old-fashioned equipment to meet the Normans near Hastings. The wall of wooden English shields could not withstand the steel of William's charging horsemen. The Norman knights profited from Hastings by making themselves lords of England. They ruled the land from strongholds called "motte-and-bailey" castles.*

BATTLE OF
STAMFORD BRIDGE

York

Humber

NORTH
SEA

NORTHUMBRIA

ENGLAND

HAROLD'S ROUTE

WALES

A MOTTE AND BAILEY CASTLE

London *Thames*

KENT

BATTLE OF SENLAC HILL

WESSEX

Bosham

Pevensey Hastings

FLANDERS

St. Valery

Somme

ENGLISH CHANNEL

NORMAN INVASION ROUTE

FRANCE

Rouen

Bayeux

Seine

Paris

BAYEUX
CASTLE

NORMANDY

THE
NORMAN
CONQUEST
A.D. 1066

SCALE   0   15   30   45 Miles

William may also have made an agreement with Harold's brother Tostig, who had been banished in disgrace from Harold's realm. Since his banishment and flight to Norway Tostig had been scheming to find a way to return to England. In September, just before William's force was ready, a Norwegian fleet appeared off the English coast. They were the Viking-prowed ships of Harold Hard-Council, King of Norway. With him came Tostig.

The news of Tostig's attack came to King Harold by a swift messenger; the first of his two fears had come to life. The Norwegian ships rowed up the Humber River, and the Norsemen poured ashore. The local leaders and men of Northumbria met them and fought with them, but were beaten. Tostig entered the city of York to place the coronet on his own head, and the Norse warriors of Harold Hard-Council grabbed whatever loot lay ready at hand.

But the next morning, quite unexpectedly, King Harold

PHOTO BY J. COMBIER

of England appeared. He met the Norsemen at Stamford Bridge, and there was a terrible battle in the old-fashioned Germanic style—the two sides hacking at each other with axes over their tall wooden shields. Harold Hard-Council was slain, and Tostig as well, and very few of the Norsemen escaped with either their plunder or their lives. King Harold's men drank deeply and ate heartily and cheered their king. Then, together with their trophies, they set off at a leisurely pace for London.

But before they had reached the city, another messenger rode to meet the King. The Normans had landed at Pevensey and were burning and robbing the countryside.

Harold wasted no time—indeed, things might have been better for him if he *had* wasted a little time to collect his forces. He hastily commanded Earl Morcar to join him with the Northumbrians, and sent out messages for a general muster of soldiers in the other shires, or counties.

In another section of the Bayeux Tapestry, *William the Conqueror is pictured arriving at the Channel on a black horse. The Viking-type long-boats are loaded to the gunwales with soldiers, horses, and the baggage of battle. Standard equipment included a kite-shaped shield, a sword worn under a coat of mail, a pointed helm over a mailed hood, and a javelin-like lance.*

The Northumbrians were slow, and the men of the western shires had a long way to come. Harold did not wait. He marched southward into Kent, and on October 13 he took up his position on a hill above the muddy valley of Senlac. On the summit was a huge, twisted apple tree, a landmark on the lonely hill, and Harold must have sent men into the highest branches to watch for the Norman host.

He set his tired men to building a scant breastwork of branches and tree trunks on the ridge, not having sufficient time to erect more permanent barriers against the Norman horsemen. He planted his two banners where everyone could see them: one was the Dragon of Wessex; the other was a gold-embroidered figure of a warrior called the Fighting Man. Harold took up his own station under the banners, and around him were set the ranks of his housecarles, his own bodyguard. The rest of his troops were placed in long lines, one rank behind the other, filling the hilltop. Then they set themselves to wait for morning and the first sight of the men from France.

A crossing of the English Channel in late September, even in a modern ship, is rough, wet, and distinctly uncomfortable. William and his heavily equipped professional soldiers made the crossing safely, but there must have been many a seasick knight or sergeant hanging his head over the side of a boat. In fact, a chronicler says that the Duke landed on the eve of September 28, and "as soon as his men were fit for service" they moved to Hastings and built a wooden fort to use as a base. It took them more than a full day to recover from that crowded, heaving trip.

Then, at last, William's scouts brought him word that Harold had taken his stand on Senlac Hill. As soon as day broke on the morning of October 14, the Duke ordered his men forward. They marched over the eight miles of gently rolling ground and came to a hill at Telham, about a mile away from the English position. The Norman knights put on their coats of mail, and the host readied itself for battle.

More than two armies faced each other that morning. This was more than just another audacious raid countered by a valiant defense. It was an invasion, launched with the purpose of changing the whole way of life of the conquered country, just as the Crusades would shortly seek to impose a new form of civilization upon the Eastern lands. Furthermore, it was a test of two different styles of warfare, one old and one new.

The English fought on foot, as they always had. The

The Normans, like the Vikings to whom they were related, were great sea voyagers. But whereas the Vikings (right) pillaged and plundered, the Normans conquered and colonized. When sea-borne warriors of that day finally reached land and after they found their footing they put on their armor (below) William is rumored to have tripped while coming ashore at Pevensey

ARCHIVES PHOTOGRAPHIQUES, AREINES

wealthier men, earls and lords, might ride to battle, but there they dismounted and stood up to their opponents, shield to shield. They were armed with battle-axes and long spears, and with the heavy double-edged sax, the sword that gave its name to the Saxon folk.

Behind the heavy-armed warriors stood the common men of the militia, most of them bare-headed, wearing only linen or leather jackets, and armed with hunting spears, Danish axes, or even clubs.

The Normans, on the other hand, were horsemen. They were professional warriors. And they were the men who, as the new conquerors of Western Europe, would go on crusade to the East. Within the Norman ranks there were also infantrymen in even greater numbers, but they were not regarded as the Normans' main striking force. The foot-men were well armed, wearing mail shirts and carrying spears and swords. Many were archers, a few had cross-bows, but most carried the clumsy Norman shortbow that drew a weight of fifty pounds. (A bow's force is measured by the amount of weight pulled horizontally when the bow-string is drawn.)

By far the most important part of the army consisted of knights and mounted soldiers, called sergeants, who galloped against the enemy with their lances leveled or their swords and axes swinging. They wore coats of mail made of mesh, thousands of tiny rings of iron riveted to-gether. These coats were split front and back so that the knight could sit his horse easily and still have his thighs protected. Hoods of mail were pulled over leather arming caps that the knights wore on their heads, and over the hoods most of them wore conical helmets with *nasals;* that is, pieces of steel that protected the nose. Their shields were kite-shaped and covered them from neck to knee. A cavalry charge by such men was an almost irresistible force. But the English, standing rank upon rank with only room between them for a man to swing his weapons, looked like an im-movable obstacle.

The Norman archers ran forward and began to shoot. There were few bows on the English side, so there was no return fire at first, and the archers probably ventured to within sixty or seventy yards. The English sheltered them-selves behind the wall of their shields. Their shields were

BIBLIOTHEQUE MUNICIPALE, ANGERS

A Saxon axeman

It was Norman horsemen, swords swinging and lances poised, who won the Battle of Hastings. As the knights charged they were protected by shields and by the soldiers with shortbows who covered their flanks (bottom right).

18

PHOTO BY J. COMBIER

BRITISH TRAVEL ASSOCIATION

Atop Senlac Ridge are the ruins of the abbey William vowed he would build if he won. The ruins overlook the bloody slope up which the Normans made their last assault.

made of linden wood, very tough and close grained, and covered with leather. And while some men must have had their arms pinned fast to their shields by occasional shots, the arrows would not penetrate the wood far enough to do much damage. The shields of the defenders were stuck full of arrows, like pincushions.

The archers came in still closer, and then suddenly the English let fly with spears, casting axes, and even great stones tied to wooden handles. The archers were driven back, and some of the foot soldiers ran up close and tried to break the front rank of the English. But they were easily scattered. When all these first attackers, like so many stinging flies, had been brushed away, Duke William stood in his stirrups to give the command to charge. Putting spurs to their horses, the mailed knights of the French rode forward. Picking up speed and momentum, they crashed into the solid mass of the shield-wall.

The knights had never met such foot soldiers before. These men did not break and scatter before the horses. They held their ground, roaring their battle chant. And with great swashing blows they cut through the chain armor, split shields, and even brought horses to the ground. The knights wavered and began to drop back, and suddenly the left wing turned and rode wildly away.

King Harold had ordered his men to hold fast at all costs. Years before, he had fought in Normandy under Duke William, and he knew well that his only chance of victory lay in his men's holding firm before the cavalry and never breaking their ranks. But now, with the knights streaming away in retreat, a crowd of militiamen ran after them in excitement, forgetting the King's orders. Duke William wheeled his men of the center division and rode down upon these militiamen and killed them all.

But the main body of the English stood fast on Senlac Hill. Once again the Normans rallied and charged. The fighting was hotter now, and heads and helmets rolled on the ground. The hill was slippery with blood and strewn with corpses, and even the well-trained Norman horses must have stumbled many times. The heavy-armed Saxons, the lords and the housecarles, planted their feet firmly and yelled their defiance of the horsemen and their cross-marked banner: "Out! Out! Holy Cross!" In this encounter King Harold's brothers Gyrth and Leofwine were slain, but in the end the Normans once again drew back.

This time William ordered one of his wings to pretend to gallop off in a panic. Again a mob of the militiamen broke ranks and chased them. Once more William turned his troops and smashed into the light-armed peasants and slaughtered them. But the Dragon of Wessex and the golden banner of the Fighting Man still stood above the English headquarters, and the shield-wall was not yet broken.

Both sides were weary, blind with sweat, bruised and bloody. The horses were lathered, the men could barely raise their arms to strike again, the string fingers of the archers were sore, and their left arms were shaky. Duke William had had three horses killed under him. Once, the word had gone around that he was slain, and he had had to push back his helmet so that the men could see his face before he could put heart back into his knights.

On the English side matters were even worse, for the arrow storm and the repeated charges were taking greater and greater toll. Then an arrow, dropping at an angle, hit King Harold in the cheek and put out his eye. In anguish, he dropped to his knees. Seeing him fall, his men lost hope. The next Norman charge burst through the shield-wall. Four knights rode to the standards, cut them down, and axed the King to death. With that the English lines, which had held so long, gave way.

Those who were left fled into the forest. Nearly the whole of the army had perished. On the Norman side the losses were enormous, although no one knows their number.

With the breaking of the shield-wall the power of the mounted warrior was supreme. Mailed cavalry, the force that William had learned to use with such success on the continent, had conquered England and was free to go on to the conquest of lands beyond the horizon.

King Harold's famous Dragon of Wessex resembled this banner. When it fell, an old order died and knighthood's triumph was secure.

STIFTSBIBLIOTHEK, ST. GALLEN

II THE VICTORIOUS FEUDAL KNIGHT

Duke William—now King William the Conqueror—was the master of a rich land, but an uneasy one. For the next five years he faced one uprising after another from stubborn and independent Saxon lords. When the rebels were at last put down, all the lands of England were owned by the Crown. William set about imposing his government on the country and giving rich estates to the adventurers who had followed his banners against King Harold. To those who cooperated with him he held out the prospect of great power and wealth; in return he received from them the pledge of military service and of personal loyalty. By doing so, he was bringing England into the unique pattern of life that made the Crusades desirable and possible.

The new pattern that the Normans brought into England is now called the feudal system. Under feudalism, only the king owned land—and even he, it was recognized, held his land from God. All other men were tenants. A man was lord of a region which he held from another man, and ultimately from the king, in exchange for the performance of a certain service, called a fee. This tight-knit relationship between a lord and his tenant, or vassal, had already spread over most of Europe; and now England was also bound in feudalism. Before many years, that feudal relationship, based on service, would find itself transported far across the sea to the Holy Land.

For warriors, feudalism meant military duty. When his lord called him, the mounted rider had to appear with his men, fully armed and ready to fight, for forty days in each year. In addition, he gave money when it was needed for special purposes, and he had to attend his lord's court and give advice or sit in judgment. If he failed in his fee, he

COURTESY OF DEAN AND CHAPTER OF DURHAM CATHEDRAL

BIBLIOTHÈQUE NATIONALE, SERVICE PHOTOGRAPHIQUE

Like so many of the crusaders, the rustic foot soldiers at left are fulfilling oaths of military service. In feudal terms they, as well as their leaders, are vassals. The leader himself doubtless swore an oath of loyalty to a higher ranking noble, perhaps upon receiving his knightly sword (above right).

23

BIBLIOTHEQUE NATIONALE

A man became the vassal of another man by appearing bare-headed before him and swearing an oath of homage. He did so in order to win protection and find employment for himself, his horse, and his sword.

forfeited his land. His children could only inherit the estate after him if they made a payment and agreed to the same conditions that their father had fulfilled.

The mailed cavalry of Europe, the riders who had destroyed King Harold's shield-wall, called themselves *chevaliers*, or horsemen. The English had a word for the free fighting men who followed a nobleman: the word *cniht*, or as it was later spelled, knight. This word came to mean the special class of armed and mounted landholders. There were other mounted men-at-arms called *serviens*, or sergeants; we may think of them as a grade below the knights, not quite so noble, not always giving military service as their fee. Both knight and sergeant were warriors. We must not imagine them to be clean-shaven, curly-headed Galahads or gentle, bright-eyed, medieval Boy Scouts, as they usually appear in romantic paintings or motion pictures. War was their trade, their livelihood, and they were generally good for nothing else.

The knights of the eleventh century were trained from childhood in the use of arms. They were taught to shoot the clumsy shortbow, to ride and wrestle, and to handle the lance, the sword, the long-hafted axe, and the mace. Training in horsemanship was vital. The knight's horse had to be taught to turn, to canter, to halt without the touch of the reins, and to stand still if its master was unseated so that he could remount. The young soldier had to wear his armor until he thought nothing of its dragging weight. A shirt of mail might weigh from twenty to thirty pounds, plus the additional weight of a padded coat, called a *gambeson*, worn under the mail. Then, there was his steel and leather helmet and his kite-shaped shield, which together added perhaps another six or seven pounds. Furthermore, he wore a belt, a scabbard, a sword, and a dagger, and carried a lance and maybe an axe, so that all in all he might be lugging more than a third of his own weight into battle. It comes as something of a shock to think what sheer hard work it must have been to fight in armor.

BIBLIOTHEQUE NATIONALE

Business agreements in the Middle Ages were written on scrolls. If mistakes were made, a knife was used to scrape away the errors.

We can think of the knight of this period as a soldier who owned a farm that was also his fort. This soldier-farmer became a knight because his lord made him one. The only ritual involved might be that his lord struck him on the shoulder, saying, "Be worthy. I make you a knight."

Knights relied upon their swords to make their way in the world, and many were consequently little better than robbers. The records are full of complaints against these mailed "devils and scoundrels."

There were, however, virtues that distinguished a knight from other men. These were simple enough, and they grew naturally out of the feudal system: courage, loyalty, and service were demanded of one who wore the armor, sword-belt, and spurs of the *chevalier*.

Without courage a man was useless in battle. Without loyalty the whole structure of the oath of fealty and the giving of homage would have fallen apart. Men had to keep their oaths and remain true to their lords. Moreover, savage as that age was, it was deeply religious, pervaded by the spirit of the Christian Church.

But in spite of the teachings of the Church and the "Truces of God" that the Church arranged, violence,

ALL: ABBEY ARCHIVES, MONTE CASSINO, PHOTOS BY SCALA, EXCEPT TOP RIGHT

Knights a-building

A lord traveling

Scribes debating

PHOTO BY ENIT

Knights feasting

A chicken being traded

Musicians playing

THE UNCOUTH FEUDAL KNIGHT

In the years before the Crusades, life in Europe was almost barbaric. Even the nobles pictured in these illustrations from an 11th-century manuscript had few comforts. Often the knights and the farm animals shared one odorous room at the base of a stone tower. Learning among the priv- *ileged class was also rare. A scribe who knew Latin had to write all communications between one isolated group and another. What little trade there was had to be carried on within the immediate feudal surroundings. But there were occasional diversions such as warfare, hunting, and music.*

ABBEY ARCHIVES, MONTE CASSINO, PHOTO BY SCALA

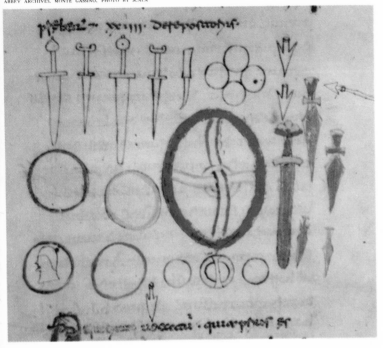

When a nobleman ordered his house-guards or knights (right) to ride forth from his castle to attack a neighbor, they put on their simple arms—the daggers or swords, spears and shields, shown at left. The knights wore cloth coats, or gambesons, *under their mail to prevent chafing; for extra protection some also wore chain mail strapped to their legs.*

battle, and murder continued. Popes spoke eloquently for peace and urged that the service demanded of the knights should include service to religion—for there were many *chevaliers* who had no scruples about stealing Church land or money, or even the golden vessels from the altar itself. It was clear that a knight must make war. That was his trade, his reason for existence. Very well then, said the Church, let him make war against the enemies of God rather than against his fellow Christians—let him carry the banner marked by a cross into the lands of the faithless.

For centuries the holy city of Jerusalem, the most sacred spot on earth to the Christian nations, had been in the hands of the Moslems. They also believed in one God, and while they agreed that both Jesus and Moses had been holy men, they claimed that Mohammed had been the greatest of God's prophets. Under his banner they had swept over the Arab lands; they had taken Persia and Syria, and in 639 they captured Palestine, called Israel today. For them Jerusalem was a sacred city too, and they made pilgrimages to its shrines, just as Christians did. Between the two religions, an uneasy peace reigned.

However, during the tenth and eleventh centuries a wilder and more warlike people began to make their power felt in the East. These were the Seljuk Turks. They began to supplant the Arabs; in the year 1071 they took

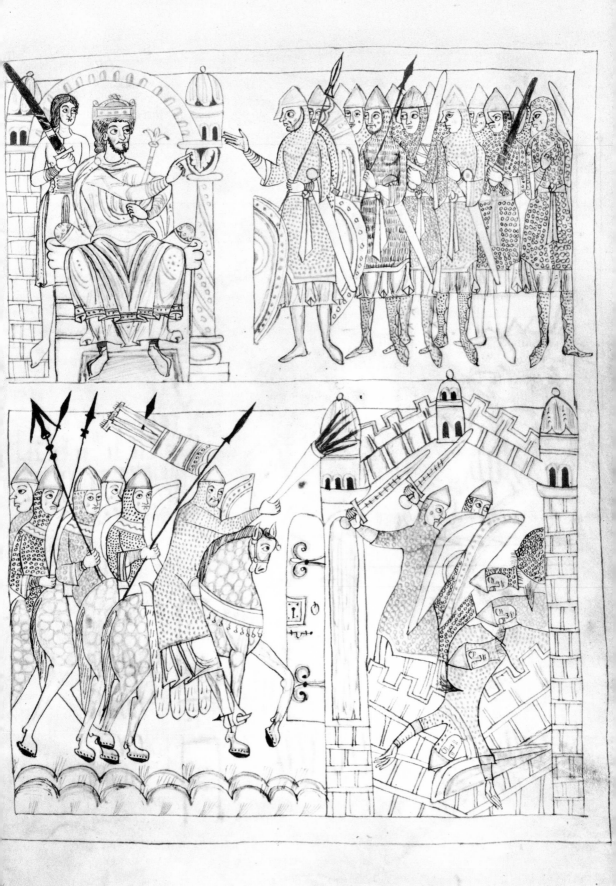

BIBLIOTHEQUE NATIONALE, SERVICE PHOTOGRAPHIQUE

bruno. eodem die inipso monaf
terro uibente papa tria intrib'
pinif cancellis facrarunt alta
ria. Tunc papa int faciido nuf
fasq; agendo. p alia falutis bo
tanita. cord epif q cardinalibuf
multozq; pfonif. huicemodi
_____ babuit ad iplin.

tutelanuq; commendauit. nifi
deo et beato Petro eiufq; iuca
rus. romanif fcilicet pontificb'
duoy numero uel ordini duina
me dignatio licet indignum af
fociauit. me olim monachum
priozenq; monafterii huuif fub
domno ac uenerabili hugone

The Church was the main source of knowledge and art. But between pope and emperor (together in a
jovial embrace below) and between churchmen and princes there were constant struggles for supremacy. French bishops are shown above at Cluny where Pope Urban won support for the First Crusade.

UNIVERSITATSBIBLIOTHEK, HEIDELBERG

Jerusalem, and during the next several years they made things difficult for the Christian pilgrims. Heavy taxes were imposed on travelers from the West, and the pilgrims were sometimes cruelly mistreated. This of itself would have upset few people except the families of the pilgrims, but the Turks and others of their wilder allies began to edge into the lands belonging to the Byzantine, or Eastern, Empire. This empire, with its rich capital city of Constantinople, occupied much of the territory now included in Greece and Turkey. The Emperor Alexius considered the authority of the Byzantine Church equal to that of the Church in Rome; yet he was concerned enough about the Turkish invasions to send to Rome for help from Pope Urban II.

And it is possible that the Pope saw the chance of performing several important feats at once if he could persuade some of the rulers of Europe to go with their knights to the aid of their fellow Christians in the East.

A victorious war in Palestine would mean the recovery of the tomb of Christ, the most revered shrine in Jerusalem. It might lead to a union between the Byzantine Christians and those who worshiped under the authority of Rome. It would strengthen the hand of the Church over all the unruly feudal princes and their followers. And, finally, it would give employment to vast numbers of quarrelsome knights who caused endless disturbances at home.

The matter came to a head in the year 1095. A council was held in the city of Clermont, in France. There the Pope proposed that war be carried into the East, to help the Byzantines and to rescue the Holy Land. The crowds were so huge that the meeting had to be held in an open field.

The Pope eloquently accused the knights of being tyrants and oppressors. He urged that every man of noble birth should take a solemn vow before a bishop that he would defend the helpless, the widows, the orphans, and that he would be the protector of womankind.

"Cast off the belt which is the symbol of your knighthood," he said angrily. "Off with it, or else go forward bravely and justify your knighthood in warring as soldiers of the Lord! Set out on this journey and you will obtain the remission of your sins and be sure of the incorruptible glory of the kingdom of heaven."

Robert the Monk, one of the chroniclers who was present at this meeting, wrote, "When Pope Urban had said this, all who were present were moved to cry out, 'It is the will of God! It is the will of God!'"

This shout became the battle cry of the First Crusade.

MUSEE DES MONUMENTS FRANCAIS, PARIS

An 11th-century pilgrim

31

III CAPTURE OF JERUSALEM

GUSTAVE DORE

Europe, at this precise moment in history, was ready for the Pope's call, like a skyrocket that only needed the touch of fire to send it roaring up. Multitudes of the poor and hungry, common people who could barely scrape a living out of the land and who were ground down by their masters, had dazzling visions of a land of milk and honey in the East. The Pope had promised that all crusaders would be free of taxes, that their debts would be forgiven, and that the journey would be the equivalent of all sorts of penances, so that their sins would be washed away. They saw themselves in their mind's eye visiting the holiest places on earth, sweeping away the infidels, since God would be on their side, and then living happily ever after in that region which the Pope called "a second Paradise of delights." They had no idea of the distances to be crossed or of the kind of country they would find. For them it would be a quick and easy journey, a battle or two, and then nothing but joy.

The same enchanting dream appealed to the knights. Many of them, even the most powerful, had been almost beggared by the endless feuds. Among them were thousands of sons whose fathers had left them nothing but debts, men whose lands had been ruined by warfare, younger sons who had no hope of inheriting anything and who saw the chance of winning rich holdings for themselves when they had chased out the Turks. The Pope had spoken directly to them when he said, "Your land is shut in on all sides by the sea and the mountains, and is too thickly populated. There is not much wealth here, and the soil scarcely yields enough to support you . . . Set out on the road to the Holy Sepulchre, take that land from the wicked people and make

The crusaders' joy on first sighting Jerusalem is dramatized in Gustave Doré's 19th-century engraving (at left). Their conquest of the Holy City was a sad contrast to the religious pageant at right. Painted by an artist at the time of the Crusades, it shows Christ in the midst of exultant knights.

LIBRERIA DEL SEMINARIO, PADOVA

JAMES ARCHER

"Dieu le veult!" *which means "God wills it!" was the emotional cry of the common people who responded to the dynamic preaching of Peter the Hermit and took the cross.*

it your own!" While a true religious impulse unquestionably stirred in many of them, there were also many who paid more attention to the merry jingle of gold pieces suggested by those words.

Their preparations could not be made rapidly, for arms and armor had to be readied, money had to be collected to pay the soldiers, leaders had to be chosen, and military plans had to be made. So it happened that the common people moved first.

The Pope had asked bishops and priests everywhere to preach the Crusade. But the most effective preaching was done by a short man with a long, homely face, a dirty, barefoot fellow from Picardy who was called Little Peter, or more often, Peter the Hermit. Riding about from place to place on a donkey that looked like his twin, he spoke with amazing eloquence; ugly as he was, he had the power to move everyone who listened to him. By April of 1096, nearly fifteen thousand people had followed him into Germany, where thousands more joined him. An advance guard of his army—which was called the People's Crusade because it consisted almost entirely of common people—set out from the city of Cologne under the leadership of a soldier of fortune named Walter the Penniless. Soon after, Peter and the main body of the crusading peasants and laborers took the road to Constantinople, whence they planned to go on to Jerusalem.

One detail had not been considered by Peter and his advisers. That was the matter of how to feed this immense rabble. Consequently, wherever they traveled they ate up the land like a mass of hungry locusts. Furthermore, a great many of those who had taken the cross—that is, had sewn onto their clothing the cross that was the badge of the war—had done so to escape their debts or taxes, to avoid being imprisoned for their crimes, or to get rich quick. Many were no better than thieves or cutthroats. Their passage through Hungary and Bulgaria, both Christian countries, was marked by the slaughter of innocent farmers, the wholesale plundering of villages and towns, and even the burning of entire cities.

They arrived on August 1 in Constantinople, where they were received patiently and kindly by the Emperor Alexius. A week later, having been shipped across the Bosporus aboard Byzantine vessels, they marched along the coast of the Sea of Marmora and settled at last near a fort called Civetot, some forty miles from Constantinople. Here they began pillaging and looting the countryside, even butchering the Christian Greeks who lived in surrounding villages. They fought constantly among themselves, and a large section split off from the leadership of Peter the Hermit and went raiding as far as the city of Nicaea. Peter went back to Constantinople to get support and supplies from the Emperor. But before he could return, the Turks had gathered troops and attacked the invaders. In a swift campaign against the crusading commoners they killed or captured all but a small number. Walter the Penniless and most of the other leaders were slain, while some of the survivors became Moslems rather

OVERLEAF: *From all over Europe nobles and common people flocked to follow the leaders of the First Crusade. The People's Crusade, led by Peter the Hermit, went overland through Hungary and met its end before reaching the Holy Land. The knights who went by sea fared better. But all passed through the gateway to the East, Constantinople.*

DAVID GREENSPAN

ENGLAND

London o

✕ Hastings

FLANDERS

Seine

Meuse

o Paris

Vezelay o

THE

HOLY ROMAN

EMPIRE

Rhine

Clermont o

FRANCE

Rhone

Aigues-
Mortes o

Marseille o

Genoa

Pisa o

CORSICA

Oder

Vistula

POLAND

Elbe

Danube

Vienna o

Budapest o

HUNGARY

Belgrad

o Venice

Zara ✕

ADRIATIC SEA

SERBIA

Rome o

Naples o

TH

*TYRRHENIAN
SEA*

NORMAN
KINGDOM
OF
SICILY

*IONIAN
SEA*

SARDINIA

SICILY

Tunis o

MEDITERRANEAN

o CITIES

✕ BATTLES AND SIEGES

0   50   100   150 Miles
SCALE

THE CRUSADES

EUROPE AND THE HOLY LAND ABOUT 1140

RUSSIAN STATES

Dnieper

Bug

Dniester

Volga

BULGARIA

BLACK SEA

THE SELJUK KINGDOM

Adrianople

Constantinople

Nicaea

Dorylaeum

YZANTINE EMPIRE

AEGEAN SEA

ARMENIA

Edessa

Tigris

Euphrates

Antioch

SYRIA

RHODES

CYPRUS

Tripoli

CRETE

Tyre

Acre

Jaffa

Damascus

THE HOLY LAND

Jerusalem

SEA

Ascalon

Damietta

Alexandria

Mansurah

Cairo

EGYPT

Nile

David Greenspan

than face death. The few who escaped got back to Constantinople where the Emperor gave them permission to remain, although because of their unruliness their weapons were taken away. The People's Crusade, begun with such high hopes, ended in blood, having accomplished nothing.

By this time, however, the first of the knightly armies was on its way. Four great divisions, under leaders famous throughout Europe, had answered the Pope's call.

First were the Frenchmen of Lorraine under Godfrey of Bouillon, Duke of Lower Lorraine. Tall and blond, he was a brave and powerful fighter, but as a leader he was inefficient and in some ways downright stupid. He was a deeply religious man, and indeed some of his followers said that his only fault was that he was too fond of prayer. His two brothers went with him. The elder, Count Eustace of Boulogne, was not very eager to leave home; but the younger, Baldwin, had made up his mind never to return from the East. He was one of those younger sons with no inheritance, and he had determined to find lands and wealth abroad.

These knights, with a large army, traveled down through Hungary and Bulgaria. They followed almost the same route that had been taken by Peter the Hermit and his horde, but their discipline was that of soldiers, and their passage was relatively swift and peaceful. By Christmas, 1096, they had reached the gates of Constantinople.

Emperor Alexius had made careful preparations for receiving the crusaders. He had arranged for provisions to be furnished them, and for squads of his imperial guards to escort them through his land to Constantinople. Knowing the customs of feudal Europe, Alexius also decided it might be wise to bind the crusaders to his service with an oath. That way, any recaptured lands formerly belonging to Byzantium would be restored to him. He had no intention of allowing his empire to be split up among these greedy barons. He planned that as each of the four crusading armies arrived, its leaders should swear fealty to him. Only then would the army be ferried across the Bosporus. Thus any temptation that might be put in their path by the sight of the splendid and rich city of Constantinople would be lessened.

When Godfrey of Bouillon arrived, trouble began at once. He refused to swear an oath of fealty to the Eastern sovereign. Also, reports had come to Godfrey that the People's Crusade had failed because of treachery on the part of the Byzantines. He had no way of knowing whether

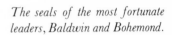

The seals of the most fortunate leaders, Baldwin and Bohemond.

Emperor Alexius of Constantinople asked for help from Rome.

these reports were true or false. He insisted that he would camp his men before Constantinople until the spring. When the Emperor stopped providing him with food, he instructed his men to take what they found in the country-side. Matters grew so tense that at one time Godfrey even sent his knights to attack the walls of the city, but they were beaten back by the Emperor's troops. In the end, Godfrey consented to take the oath. He swore to acknowledge Emperor Alexius as lord of any land that might be taken and to hand over to him any land which had previously belonged to Byzantium. Then his troops were sailed across to the Asian coast where they made their camp near the city of Nicomedia.

Close behind Godfrey came the second great crusading army. This one was made up of Normans from southern Italy and Sicily. Driven by the same restlessness and avarice that had sent some of their people with Duke William into England, these Normans had long before traveled into

Godfrey of Bouillon, leader of the first crusading army, is shown below preparing to sail to the East, as confident as William the Conqueror. In fact, Godfrey's ship looked more like one of William's boats than does this fanciful, over-crowded 14th-century vessel.

NATIONAL BIBLIOTHEK, VIENNA

the pleasant southern country and made themselves its dukes.

This army, led by Bohemond of Taranto, sailed across the Adriatic instead of taking the land route. With great difficulty it climbed the Albanian mountains and then marched across northern Greece and on to Constantinople. With true Norman craft, Bohemond pretended to be exceedingly friendly to Byzantium and so managed matters that Alexius gave him a rich gift of gold and jewels. He took the oath of loyalty eagerly and with every show of readiness, and his army in turn was sent over the Bosporus.

That very day the third of the leaders arrived with his men from southern France, from the region known as Provence. This was Count Raymond IV of Toulouse. Raymond was close to sixty years of age. Like most of his Provençal countrymen, he was haughty and stubborn, but he was a man of his word. He did not wish to be treated *The armies set up camps on the* like the other lords. His blood was so noble, he said, *way; the nobles' tents in the center.* that in his own land he was the equal of any king. In

Das Mittelalterliche Hausbuch

BIBLIOTHEQUE NATIONALE

Some of the knights took their families with them on the overland route in rough wagons. This particular wagon has a flower-throwing lady aboard.

consequence, he would not become the vassal of a mere emperor.

The other leaders of the Crusade begged him to give in, and Godfrey of Bouillon urged him to compromise rather than harm the Christian cause. Finally, Count Raymond agreed to swear a modified oath. He promised never to wage war against Byzantium and to see that nothing was done by himself or his men to harm the Emperor. This type of oath was often taken by vassals in southern France, and Alexius was satisfied with it. It is noteworthy that of all the crusading leaders, Raymond was the only one who emerged from the war with the reputation of being a man who kept his promises.

His army joined the other two. Then the fourth great host arrived from Europe. It came in two sections. The first, consisting of men from Flanders under Count Robert II, reached Constantinople in December. The second, and larger, division was led by Duke Robert of Normandy, the eldest son of William the Conqueror. He was a mild and courteous man who shared the command with Stephen of Blois, his brother-in-law. Stephen, who was extremely rich and loved his luxuries, had been shamed into going by his wife. This army of Normans, English, and Bretons did not arrive at Constantinople until May, 1097. Both of them took the oath and received magnificent presents from Alexius. Stephen wrote his wife, who was the daughter of Duke William: "Your father, my dear, is a generous man, but he is nothing compared to the Emperor!" Then they were sent to join the other crusaders in Asia.

Emperor Alexius must have breathed a long sigh of relief when they left. He had asked the West for help, but he had not expected these four immense armies to come in; nor had he expected fellow Christians to be so rude.

Now the combined armies of the cross, numbering per-

PERMISSION OF THE TRUSTEES OF THE BRITISH MUSEUM

The walls and towers of Nicaea

41

batailles tusques a · deconfite. Li autre sen et · q̃ ses se contenoient
puus vsurent toutes · maienent mour. Il guen · flaprocha uit la l
cvmme qui estoit bui · a cele pur · o toute sa bataill · buymont qui nest
uessies fier chapleis · le. Et si feri mour uigne · encote assamblee
· uisement . Lors en deou · bla alui . ant pot

haps thirty-five thousand men on foot and horse, prepared for their first battles against the infidel. If the Turks, after having wiped out the rabble of the People's Crusade, thought they would have as easy a victory over this army, they were at once to be disappointed.

The first encounter was before the walls of the ancient city of Nicaea, only a short distance from Constantinople, on the road heading southeast to Jerusalem. The crusaders prepared to besiege the city, whereupon Sultan Kilij Arslan, ruler of that region, sent an army against them. The Turks were no match for the heavy cavalry of the West and they were driven off with great losses. The city was taken—but it surrendered to Emperor Alexius. His men had secretly gained admission and arranged the surrender, planting the flag of Byzantium on the walls. The crusaders, who had already forgotten their oath to Alexius and had been looking forward to rich booty for themselves, felt that they had been tricked.

The real test of their strength came on the first day of July, 1097. They had split up into two columns about two miles apart but out of touch with each other. The first column, led by Bohemond of Taranto, came out into a wide plain not far from the ruins of an old city called Dorylaeum. Here they were suddenly attacked by a vast host of Turkish horsemen. This was the whole force of Kilij Arslan—thousands upon thousands of men ready to avenge the fall of Nicaea.

All of them were mounted upon swift horses capable of greater speed than the heavy chargers, or *destriers*, of the crusaders. They wore almost no armor and carried short bows and curved swords. Their manner of fighting was enough to drive the knights half mad, for they dashed up, shot their arrows, and galloped away again. Riding after them was like chasing a swarm of bees with a club. Soon the knights drew back and closed their ranks. Their way of fighting was to meet the enemy head on, but they could not make the Turks stand and fight; they could only defend themselves. Their horses were killed under them and their shields were split by hundreds of arrows. The infantry could not stand against the swift rushes of the Turks.

ABBEY ARCHIVES, MONTE CASSINO, PHOTO BY SCALA

The river surrounding this Syrian city greatly impressed an early traveler.

The first victory against the Turks was the Battle of Dorylaeum, represented in this miniature by a colorful clash of knights beneath the tiled and gilded walls of the city. In reality, Dorylaeum was a humble town, the junction of the trade routes south and east to Jerusalem. The tents of the opposing armies (shown on either side of the battle) were actually many miles apart.

LA BIBLIOTECA NACIONAL, MADRID

When the crusaders could not batter down or undermine a city wall (see back end sheet), they rolled up siege

towers to carry men over the battlements. Note the Saracen archer's scale armor of overlapping metal plates.

Bohemond and his nephew Tancred, Robert of Flanders, and Robert of Normandy charged out time and again, only to be surrounded by Turkish cavalrymen. They fought their way clear, but the situation seemed hopeless.

Meanwhile, messengers from Bohemond had found the second column of the army, led by Duke Godfrey and Count Raymond. Godfrey soon arrived on a ridge above the Turks, who were now closing in for the kill. He thundered down the hill with his knights. Behind him, taking all possible shortcuts, swept Count Raymond's army. Bohemond at once rallied his weary troops. Within moments the Turks, who had thought they had the entire Western army surrounded, were scattered. The crusaders rode through them and over them; they chased them and killed hundreds more, cutting them down in the saddle from behind. The camp of the Sultan was captured, and so great was the panic that three days after they marched away from the battlefield, the crusaders still found the corpses of horses lying by the roadside—the Turks, in their terror to escape, had ridden them to death.

The Battle of Dorylaeum was a great, if an accidental, victory. And from this time on, the crusaders realized that their enemies were worthy of much respect. The Turks, who came to be called Saracens in the same general way that all European crusaders were called Franks, would have many chances to convince the crusaders of their bravery before Jerusalem was reached.

Taking fresh horses from the captured Turks, the crusaders moved on. They were heading south toward Syria and the great city of Antioch, which they had to take to protect the road behind them when they marched to Jerusalem. The Christian population of many towns on their way welcomed them, and the Turks melted away instead of trying to fight. But the heat and thirst were greater enemies than the Moslems.

When they reached the town of Marash, some one hundred miles from Antioch, Baldwin, Godfrey's younger brother, turned aside to the east. His reason, he said, was that thus he could defend the flank of the army. Actually, he was looking for less wearying lands to conquer for himself.

He found them in Armenia. Under the pretext of freeing Armenians from Turkish rule, he made himself master of the countryside. With a combination of brutal force and pure trickery, he became, at last, the prince of Edessa and the ruler of a rich and powerful state. Thus one leader of the Crusade found the wealth he had come for.

The crusaders used either the money of Byzantium (shown below) or imitations of Saracen coins (above).

COIN GALLERIES, INC. N.Y.

Monuments de la Monarchie Française, BY MONTFAUCON

BELLVM AM TE ISC L NIA IV

Kerbogha (shown at right in this window painting) is hit by Robert of Normandy.

The rest of the joint army arrived before the walls of Antioch late in October and sat down to besiege the city. The walls were too strong to be breached and the city too large to be surrounded by the crusaders. On the other hand, its garrison was small. Day followed day with assaults that were beaten back. Winter pressed on the army. Where before they had gone thirsty, now they were constantly wet and chilled by rain. Food began to run short. Bohemond went to find provisions and was ambushed by a large number of Turks. With hard fighting he drove them off, but his own men were too weakened and weary to collect provisions afterward.

Bohemond, the Norman leader of the second crusading army, had already decided that Antioch was to be his own prize. Remembering the example of Emperor Alexius at Nicaea, he determined to plant his own banner first upon the walls so that no one could dispute his claim to the city. He secretly made contact with a Moslem Armenian within the city, a captain named Firouz, who agreed to open one of the towers to him. When all was ready, Bohemond called the other captains of the Crusade together and told them his plan.

At sunset on June 2, 1098, the army marched away from

BIBLIOTHEQUE NATIONALE, SERVICE PHOTOGRAPHIQUE

the city as if going off on an expedition. But when it was dark they returned. Sixty of Bohemond's knights climbed a ladder outside the Tower of the Two Sisters and were admitted by Firouz. They quickly took over two further towers, while Bohemond himself climbed into the city. Some men ran along the walls to capture new towers, and others opened two of the great gates. The crusaders poured into the city. When that day ended, the only Turks left alive were a few who had taken refuge in the citadel that stood apart from the walls and was too strong to be stormed. Bohemond's banner waved, as he had planned, from the highest point of the walls.

But all the fighting was not yet done. The Moslem chieftain Kerbogha came down with a huge army and surrounded the Franks within the city they had just taken. For four weeks the crusaders suffered from near starvation and constant assault.

Then a man named Peter Bartholomew came to see Count Raymond of Toulouse and Bishop Adhemar, the papal legate. Peter claimed that Saint Andrew had appeared to him in a vision and had revealed the hidden location of the very lance that had pierced the side of Christ when He was crucified. Despite many doubts, a rusty iron lance head was indeed found in that spot, and the crusaders regarded it as a divine sign. With this relic in their possession, the spirits of the Franks rose.

On the morning of June 28 they drew up in their divisions, with the lance held before them, and marched out of the gates. Kerbogha had not realized how many of them there were. Before he could send his soldiers against them, they had almost filled the plain in front of him. The Turks tried their usual tactics of riding up to shoot and then darting away again. Godfrey of Bouillon and both Roberts —the Count of Flanders and the Duke of Normandy—were able to push after them in good order. Bohemond held the rear, and in spite of terrible losses, kept the Turks at bay. Unable to outflank the Christians, and unable to face the repeated charges of their heavy-armed knights, Kerbogha turned and fled. His whole army began to break up and re-

The Battle of Jerusalem, as painted by a 14th-century miniaturist, shows both the life of Christ (upper windows) and the fight itself. The crusaders, having rallied from their tents and rolled up a siege tower, are about to storm the walls. The artillery (below at right) is firing up a rain of rocks from the counter-weighted trebuchet. At times these slinging machines sent more grisly objects, such as mutilated corpses, into a besieged city.

BIBLIOTHEQUE NATIONALE, SERVICE PHOTOGRAPHIQUE

An Arab at the time of the Crusades dressed in his flowing robes.

treat in panic. The crusaders pursued them, slaying great numbers and scattering the rest. "We returned to Antioch with great joy," a knightly chronicler wrote, "praising and blessing God, who had given victory to His people."

Count Raymond felt that the city should be held by Emperor Alexius (although it was he who, as leader of the third army, had given the Emperor the most trouble about the oath). But in spite of all opposition, and in spite of that oath, Bohemond felt that Antioch was his—he had fought for it and by his plan had taken it. The others finally gave in, and he was left in possession of the city. Thus a second of the leaders of the Crusade found his goal.

Count Raymond now regarded himself as commander-in-chief of the combined armies. He marched on toward Jerusalem and came to the town of Arqa, which he besieged. He was joined by Count Robert of Flanders and Godfrey of Bouillon, and quarrels at once began among them and their men over the leadership of the Crusade.

From city to city they went into Palestine, now starving and thirsty, now coming to regions where there were lush gardens and towns full of wine, bread, cheese, and oil. The army grew smaller as men died, or lost heart and went home, or stopped to hold towns for themselves. At last, on June 7, 1099, a year after the fall of Antioch and nearly three years after the start of the Crusade, the army had reached its goal. Before the crusaders lay the holy city of Jerusalem, high on its hills and surrounded by strong old walls and towers.

The Moslems had blocked up or poisoned the wells around the city and had driven away all the herds and flocks. In spite of hunger and heat, thick dust, and the fact that they had to go six miles to get water to drink, the armies of the West besieged the city. They built wooden, wheeled towers that could be rolled close to the walls. These were protected by fresh hides of oxen and camels so that the Greek fire—blazing masses of pitch and sulphur and other chemicals—thrown at them from the city would not set them aflame. Other siege engines were used: catapults, like giant crossbows, which shot stones and enormous arrows; mangonels, which were long beams that swung up and hurled stones over the walls; trebuchets, which were great slings that worked by counterweights.

On July 10 the moving towers were pushed up close to the walls, and a few days later a fierce assault was made against two main sectors. Here is the eye-witness account by that same knightly chronicler:

Before we attacked, our bishops and priests preached to us and commanded that all men should go in procession in honor of God around the ramparts of Jerusalem. . . . Early on Friday we made a general attack but were unable to do anything and fell back in great fear. Then at the approach of the hour at which Our Lord Jesus Christ suffered for us upon the cross [about nine in the morning], our knights in one of the wooden towers made a hot attack, with Duke Godfrey and Count Eustace among them. One of our knights, named Letold, clambered up the wall. As soon as he was there, the defenders fled along the walls and down into the city, and we followed them, slaying them and cutting them down as far as the Temple of Solomon, where there was such slaughter that our men waded in blood up to their ankles.

Nowhere better than in this terrible battle can the contradictions within the crusading spirit be seen. For the knight goes on: "The crusaders ran about the city, seizing gold, silver, horses, mules, and pillaging the houses filled with riches. Then, happy and weeping with joy, our men went to adore the sepulchre of Our Lord, and rendered up the offering they owed. The following morning we climbed to the roof of the Temple and fell upon the Sara-

UNIVERSITY LIBRARY, EDINBURGH

The Turks and all Moslems throughout the East considered the capture of Jerusalem a disaster. Above is an Arab view of the Temple's destruction.

51

UNIVERSITATSBIBLIOTHEK, HEIDELBERG

Everywhere triumphant, the crusaders stormed Saracen fortresses.

cens who were there, men and women, beheading them with our swords."

The Christians had indeed triumphed. But even before the attack, an important election had taken place to determine which of the leaders should govern Jerusalem. Of those who had started out, four major figures were left: Godfrey of Bouillon, who had led the first great crusading army; Raymond of Toulouse, leader of the third army; and the two leaders of the fourth army, Robert of Normandy and Robert of Flanders. Young Tancred, who had led the second army with Bohemond of Taranto, had made himself ruler of the city of Bethlehem, and in any case he had too small a following to be given so important a post.

Now that the city had been won, the two Roberts wanted only to return to Europe. They gave their backing to Godfrey. Count Raymond, in utter fury, found that even his own followers would not support him as a candidate. Thus in the end it was Godfrey who ruled Jerusalem. He would not be king in the city where Christ had died. Instead he took the title of Advocate of the Holy Sepulchre.

He was not to reign long. Almost at once he plunged into a quarrel with Count Raymond, which ended with the Count marching northward into Syria to see if he could find territory of his own there.

In July, 1100, Godfrey fell ill with typhoid fever, probably from eating fresh fruit at a banquet. When he died there were two possible successors to his place. One was Bohemond, conqueror of Antioch; the other, Godfrey's younger brother, Baldwin.

But Bohemond, knowing nothing of Godfrey's death, had left Antioch and gone into the hills to deal with a strong force of Turks who threatened the country of Melitene, which he hoped to annex. He was ambushed and captured. He cut off a lock of his yellow hair and sent it by a messenger to Baldwin, who was still ruling in Edessa. Count Baldwin set out at once with a small force, but the Turks retreated before him and got away, carrying Bohemond into imprisonment. When Baldwin returned to his own city, the news came to him of the death of his brother Godfrey. With his household and a strong bodyguard, Baldwin traveled at once to Jerusalem, where he was received with joy. He had none of the reluctance of Godfrey to wear a crown in that city where Christ had been crowned with thorns. On Christmas Day, 1100, he became the king of Jerusalem. To this penniless younger brother, the Crusade had brought all he desired and more.

BIBLIOTECA VATICANA

BIBLIOTHEQUE NATIONALE, SERVICE PHOTOGRAPHIQUE

The sacred shrines of Jerusalem (left) were in Christian hands by 1099. The knights secured their conquest · by taking the remaining coastal cities. Painted into the scene of the capture of Ascalon, below, are siege weapons of the 15th century, such as the "bombards," or early cannons.

RHEIMS CATHEDRAL, PHOTO BY GIRAUDON

MUSEE DES MONUMENTS FRANCAIS, PARIS

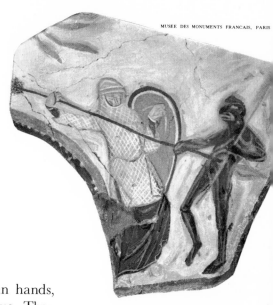

IV THE CROSS BELEAGUERED

A popular religious art subject was that of spearing the Devil; the crusaders believed that killing Saracens was equally good for the soul.

Now that Jerusalem was once again in Christian hands, many knights felt obliged to live up to a new virtue. They had won a holy war, they had rescued the holy places, and now they set themselves high tasks worthy of their knighthood.

Religious orders were formed that were to play an important part in the history of knighthood. Partly religious and partly military, they bound their members together in a kind of mystical brotherhood. Nothing, it seemed, could be better than to be one of a band of loving comrades-in-arms, sworn to uphold noble ideals, dedicated to the knight's greatest joy—battle—and certain that with death one would enter paradise.

The first of these orders was said to have been established by Godfrey of Bouillon himself when he became ruler of Jerusalem. He ordered that there should be twenty canons of the Holy Sepulchre, monks whose duty was to guard the tomb of Christ. At once a great many of the crusaders swore obedience to the prior of this order and took upon themselves the duties of defending the Holy Sepulchre. In time they became known as "the most worthy"; the white surcoats of the Knights of the Holy Sepulchre, masked with the red cross of Jerusalem, were seen in the forefront of many battles, where they fought under a white banner speckled with red drops signifying the Holy Blood.

A few years later the Order of the Knights of St. John,

The knights of the Second Crusade were impelled by a religious zeal that at first seemed even stronger than their lust for new conquests and further riches. They bowed willingly to the discipline of the medieval Church.

better known as the Hospitallers, was established. It was named after the Hospital—or hostel—of St. John, which had been founded to provide a refuge for the few pilgrims who came to Jerusalem under Turkish rule. After the First Crusade the hospital had a rush of new visitors, and the new order of monks cared for them.

Many of the monks were knights who wanted to atone for their wicked deeds or who felt the call of religion now that they had rescued Jerusalem. This order soon became a military one, more knightly than monkish. Its members lived as simply as monks and took vows of chastity, poverty, and obedience. They owned nothing, wore plain clothes, and were to live on bread and water. But in battle they dressed again in their armor, girded on their swords, and fought like the knights they really were. They wore black robes with a white cross of eight points over their hearts.

Godfrey, now widely revered for his piety, gave the Hospitallers his estates in the Low Countries. Other nobles made them equally rich gifts. The order grew to be one of the strongest in the world, with churches and manors, fortresses and lands, in Europe as well as in the East.

Soon after the founding of the Hospitallers, another great knightly order was formed: the Templars. They originated when two knights, Hugh of Payens and Geoffrey of St. Aldemar, swore to be the protectors of pilgrims who voyaged to the Holy Land. Other knights and sergeants banded with them, and in the year 1128 they were confirmed as a regular order and allowed to wear a white robe emblazoned with a red cross.

The Templars were given their name because of the building they received as headquarters, the so-called Temple of Solomon. It was that same building on the rooftop of which so many unfortunate Moslem men and women had been massacred. Its dome and columns appeared on the Templars' seal. Through contributions of money and lands from kings and barons, the Templars soon became as rich as Solomon had been, and almost as proud. Their influence upon the whole of knighthood was immense.

In the beginning their rules were very strict. They exiled themselves from their homes and swore to fight to the death for the holy places of Christendom. They were to attend mass at least three times a week. They were to accept every combat, no matter how outnumbered they were, and to ask no quarter and give none. They were soon dreaded beyond all others by the Moslems. Although the order itself was rich, its members owned nothing but their weapons. They

BIBLIOTHEQUE NATIONALE, SERVICE PHOTOGRAPHIQUE

Many myths grew up around Godfrey. One was that he could cut off a camel's head with a single blow.

COURTESY OF ROGER SHERMAN LOOMIS

BIBLIOTHEQUE NATIONALE, SERVICE PHOTOGRAPHIQUE

Godfrey (above, at right) was regarded as one of history's nine heroes. Another ideal knight was the fabled Roland. While fighting against the Moors in Spain (left), he died rather than summon help.

57

were, in fact, like the Hospitallers, both monks and knights at the same time; but as the years went by, the Templars began to acquire a reputation for arrogance and haughtiness.

Their hard rules had been given to them by Bernard of Clairvaux, later famed as Saint Bernard. He was one of the most striking figures of the whole age, and one who was to be responsible for the second major Crusade into the East.

He was a proud, stern man, full of passionate love for his religion, who let nothing stand in his way when he thought he was right. His name was renowned throughout Europe, and his power was greater than that of many kings. His sponsorship of the Templars meant not only that many knights would flock to join that order but also that eyes would turn more often to the kingdom of Jerusalem and to the rewards to be won by fighting against the infidel.

There was indeed good reason for men's eyes to turn to the Holy Land, for there were rumblings of trouble coming from that unquiet spot. The feudal states that had been established there had come upon hard times since their founding in the First Crusade. They were now a prize to be fought over by their own subjects, as well as by the surrounding Moslems. Warfare had been continuous for over forty years.

Then the news came to Europe that the Turks had attacked Edessa, capital of the state Count Baldwin had first taken for himself. The city had been conquered and most of its Christian inhabitants killed. The whole principality was once again in the possession of the Moslems.

A new crusade was needed. Clearly, Bernard of Clairvaux was the one man to preach it.

He spoke in an open field outside the town of Vézelay in France on March 31, 1146, fifty-one years after that stirring speech made by Pope Urban which had set in motion the First Crusade. Bernard's voice carried to the whole immense crowd as he called upon the people to go to war—this time not for land or riches, but in penance for their many sins. Before he had finished, the thousands there were shouting, "Crosses—give us crosses!" Bernard and his monks tore off their dark habits and cut them into crosses on the spot. The women sewed the crosses onto their men's tunics and willingly waved them off to war.

ARCHIVIO DI STATO, VENICE

Men were expected to attend mass at least once a day; a knight at prayer (above) was as common a sight as a knight on horseback. When they reached the Holy Land, many crusaders joined the new religious orders—both from piety and from a desire to fight. The colorful Teutonic knight at right is pictured with his helmet and shield close at hand.

UNIVERSITATSBIBLIOTHEK, HEIDELBERG

BIBLIOTECA DEL MONASTERIO DE EL ESCORIAL, MADRID

Soon he was able to write to the pope that "villages and towns are now deserted. You will scarcely find one man for every seven women." Among those who answered his appeal were many great barons of France. They were led by King Louis VII, whose knights, at first unwilling to leave the country with him, were now as eager as he himself.

Bernard then went to Germany, which was included, along with northern Italy, in that realm called the Holy Roman Empire. There the German king, Conrad III, was cool to the idea of going off to the distant East to do his fighting. But Bernard, preaching to the King and speaking as though he were God himself, cried out, "Man, what should I, your God, have done for you that I have not done?" Conrad agreed to take the cross and accepted the banner that Bernard tore from the altar of the church and gave to him.

Thus began a holy war that was sadly doomed from the start.

Louis and Conrad started out separately, and after battles along the way with both the Turks and the Byzantines, they met in the Holy Land at Acre in June, 1148. There they held council with the local nobles: King Baldwin III of Jerusalem, the grand masters of the Templars and Hospitallers, and many other leaders. The decision was made to attack the city of Damascus.

A strong army was put into the field, the mightiest the Franks had ever marshaled. It consisted of the French, the Germans, and the troops of the various barons of

The greatest spiritual force in 12th-century Europe was Saint Bernard. He bullied kings, placated emperors, and preached the Second Crusade (right). Although he never went to the Holy Land, he was deeply interested in the military orders established there. Some of the duties of the Hospitallers (caring for the sick, guiding pilgrims, hunting, exorcising evil spirits) are pictured at left.

Outline of Christianity

Palestine. They marched to Damascus, which had very strong walls manned by battle-seasoned Turks, and immediately besieged the city. Then, in their customary fashion, they spent most of their time arguing over who was to have Damascus when they had taken it. While they were thus haggling over spoils they had not yet won, a powerful Turkish force was marching to the relief of the city.

In the face of this threat the local nobles suddenly decided that the campaign against Damascus had been a mistake. They persuaded the two European kings to give up the siege, and within a few months the entire Crusade was abandoned. It had accomplished nothing but the loss of thousands of lives, mostly by sickness and Turkish snipers.

After this dreadful failure, Bernard of Clairvaux, grief-stricken, said, "The Lord, provoked by our sins, has judged the world with justice but not with his usual mercy. . . ."

That humiliation of the Christians was not yet completed. There appeared among the Moslems a young man whose fame was to be as great in the West as in the East—Saladin, Sultan of Egypt and Syria. Under his rule the

BOTH: MUSÉE DES MONUMENTS FRANÇAIS, PARIS

A Templar, wielding his banner, bursts into the scene above with all the naïve enthusiasm of the knights who came from Europe to join the Second Crusade. The local barons, who had begun to make a comfortable and profitable life for themselves in Palestine, were considerably less

Moslem world experienced the same upsurge of unifying faith that had fired Europe.

Saladin was clever enough to begin his campaign against the Christians by arranging a truce with King Baldwin. That gave him time to rally the Moslem nations while the Christian leaders, bent on further glory, quarreled among themselves. When he had prepared his campaign against Palestine, the region surrounding Jerusalem, all he needed was a slight excuse to break the truce.

The incident was soon provided by one of those younger sons who, since he had no inheritance in France, had come to the Holy Land to seek his fortune. His name was Reynald of Châtillon, Lord of Outer Jordan.

The truce between Saladin and Baldwin provided that Christian and Moslem merchants could cross each other's territory, and Reynald could not suppress his excitement at the sight of so many rich caravans passing almost under his nose. At last he could hold off no longer; he swooped down on a large caravan and robbed it of everything it carried.

enthusiastic about the Crusade and the prospect of fighting Sultan Nur ed-Din. The anxious faces peering out from this walled city at the departing crusaders may represent the barons, whose loyalty to the cause of the cross was weakened even further by bribes offered by the ruler of Damascus.

ويحمل الفص والجباله والفس والابله انها ضعفت على بالزر فاضاعت بعض ما اربحا

ونشدد ما اربحا لما اتى موت بالرقعة درهما وقطعة دفعت لها ان رغبت فى المستوفى المعلم

واشرت الى الدرهم فوبخ بالسر المفهم وان ابن اراد ان تخذى فخذى القطعة وايمرخت

نات الى انخفاض البدر بالتم والابلغ الهم وقالت دع جدك لك ينبع عابد لك فاسقطه

طلع الشيخ بلدنه والشعر وايح برده فتبان ان الشيخ من اهل يروج وهو الذى وفى

Saladin swore to have revenge. In September, 1183, he crossed the Jordan River and entered Palestine with an army but could not lure the Franks out to do battle with him. The stalemate ended in another truce which was broken almost at once by Reynald. The caravan he attacked this time was said to be carrying fine goods for Saladin's own sister. Now Saladin could not be stopped.

He concentrated his troops on the frontier. The Franks gathered a huge army under Guy of Lusignan, who had succeeded to the throne of Jerusalem on the death of King Baldwin. With them went the Bishop of Acre carrying the most holy of relics, the True Cross on which Christ had died.

Saladin's host was camped near the Sea of Galilee, a broad lake, with many of his men on the hills round about. The Franks, marching toward them, camped upon the dry and rocky heights of a pass called, from its two peaks, the Horns of Hattin. By the time the King's banner was set up, his soldiers were suffering terribly from thirst. Their condition was made worse by the sight of the water shimmering below them.

The Moslems set fire to the dry grass and began their assault. The Christian infantry, staggering with thirst, broke up and fell before the arrows of the Turks. The knights fought desperately, retreating up the hill to rally around King Guy's banner. Time after time the Moslems charged; the Christians were surrounded, unable to retreat, too weak to fight back. At last the King's tent and his banner were thrown down. The knights dropped their swords, slipped from their horses, and fell exhausted to the ground. The Moslems ran in and took them captive. Many were unhurt; it was fatigue that had defeated them, and heat and thirst, not wounds.

ISRAEL GOVERNMENT TOURIST OFFICE

The True Cross was captured, and King Guy and so many other prisoners were taken that it was said you could buy a Christian slave for the price of a pair of sandals. Saladin himself cut off the head of Reynald, and he ordered that the two hundred Templars and Hospitallers be executed. But to the other barons and to King Guy he was as courteous as a knight should be. He sent them on to

At the end of the Second Crusade the Moslem world was united under a new leader, Saladin. He led his men, who looked much like the jubilant Arabs shown at left, to the hills bordering the Sea of Galilee. There, at the Horns of Hattin (framing a view of the sea, above), they fought their conclusive battle with the beleaguered armies of the cross.

BÜRGERBIBLIOTHEK, BERN

Imptr allofa cıue
Salerni.

Damascus where they were held for ransom. This terrible Christian defeat made Saladin master of the Holy Land.

Swiftly he took each of the fortress-cities in turn: Tiberias, Acre, Jaffa, Ascalon. At last he stood before Jerusalem. There was no hope for those within the city, and on October 2, 1187, they surrendered.

Saladin's entrance into Jerusalem was quite different from that of the Christians when they had taken it from the Moslems eighty-eight years before. Not a building was burned this time, not a person injured, and nothing was stolen. The Moslems had agreed to let the Christian inhabitants ransom themselves for ten gold pieces per man, five for a woman, and one for a child. For seven thousand of the poorer folk who could not raise the whole ransom, Saladin accepted thirty thousand gold pieces instead of seventy thousand. But there were thousands of the poor who could pay nothing. Patriarch Heraclius, head of the Christian Church in Jerusalem, and other wealthy churchmen paid their ten gold pieces per man and left the city with wagonloads of gold, silver, and precious stones. Behind them trudged the poor who, unable to pay, had to become slaves of the Moslems.

Saladin's brother, al-Adil, was so touched by the sight that he begged for the liberty of a thousand of them as a reward for the fighting he had done. This was granted. Saladin himself freed all the old people and gave money from his own treasury for the widows and orphans of knights and sergeants killed in battle. He granted freedom to five hundred more for the sake of the captain of the city, and he gave seven hundred to the Patriarch, who was thus able to save his gold. Saladin's chivalry, and that of many of his officers, put to shame the behavior of the Christian knights.

As the long procession of Christians, free and captive, moved away from Jerusalem, the golden banner of Saladin was raised above the walls. The cross upon the Dome of the Rock, the mosque that the Christians had made into a church, was pulled down. The very statues, wrote a Christian chronicler, wept for shame. The Eastern kingdom of the Franks had crashed into ruin.

The fate of civilians in a city besieged during the Middle Ages was invariably unhappy. Women and children (left) were not spared war's cruelties. But when the Saracens reconquered Jerusalem, they showed more mercy than the crusaders had and even freed many of the Christian citizens.

The knights on the right in the battle scene below still wear the old Norman helmet; those charging into the scene from the left have completely covered their heads and faces with the new closed helm that came into use at the time of the Third Crusade (1190). But both sides are shown engaged in the same style of free-swinging warfare that characterized all the early Crusades.

THE PIERPONT MORGAN LIBRARY

In the richly decorated courts of the East the crusaders found a deeper respect for learning than in Europe.

V THE TWO CHAMPIONS

After almost a century of fighting, methods of warfare had not basically changed. Knights still preferred the heavy cavalry charge, lances leveled, swords swinging; and when they could catch the Moslems, they overwhelmed them. Chain mail had grown a little heavier, helmets more closed, and shields smaller. But weapons were used in the same effective way.

The war in the East had some effect on siegecraft and fortress building. In Asia the crusaders found stone citadels larger and stronger than almost anything to be found in Europe; therefore they developed mightier siege engines. Most of these machines were simply more elaborate versions of ancient Roman devices. Battering rams protected by wooden roofs, or penthouses, wheeled towers such as those that had been built for the taking of Jerusalem, mangonels for slinging stones, catapults for casting rocks or six-foot-long arrows, ballistas for hurling pots of Greek fire or javelins or stone bullets—all these were dragged about by armies in the field, or more often, the timbers and ropes were lugged about and the machines constructed on the spot.

The knights who settled in the Holy Land learned to appreciate some of the luxuries they had gaped at when they first came. They built superb castles, like the Hospitallers'

BIBLIOTHÈQUE NATIONALE, SERVICE PHOTOGRAPHIQUE

famous Krak of the Chevaliers near Tripoli in northern Palestine. They softened the chambers of cold stone with fine hangings and colorful carpets. They learned to wear the turbans and comfortable flowing robes of the Saracens and brought the styles back to Europe with them. They developed a taste for spices in their food, and they began to discover that leisure time—if there was any—could be used for enjoyment instead of for fighting.

Yet the greatest result of the early Crusades was more difficult to see than armaments or castles. It had really begun long before with the idea that a knight must be not only brave and loyal but godly as well. Now there had come a further change in manners. It was felt that knighthood carried with it a quality that can only be described as courtesy. A knight must be brave in battle, but he must also be brave in spirit. Instead of riding over a fallen foe, he must raise him to his feet. Instead of throwing a noble prisoner into a dungeon, he must treat him nobly. To some degree this change had come because of contact with the Moslems. The Christian knights, particularly those who settled in the Holy Land, must have felt the desire to behave at least as honorably and politely as the princes of the infidels did.

Many times during sieges there were duels of honor between warriors from either side, and the fighting would stop while everyone watched. Invitations to feasts and entertainments were given as Christians and Moslems grew to know each other. When, in 1190, Acre was besieged by the Franks, the fighting was often interrupted by more friendly exchanges, and once a mock battle was held between the Christian boys and the boys of the Saracen camp.

What had developed was the concept of chivalry. Chivalry became the ideal of knighthood, a way of living and thinking that should distinguish the knight from lesser men. It included the earlier concepts of courage and loyalty, the idea of feudal service, and the later development of religious service; it also included upright behavior and courteous deeds. In a way it was like the distinction we make today between an athlete—one who devotes himself to playing a certain game or competes in physical skills— and sportsmanship, which is the right behavior for such a man. You might say that the knight was the athlete, and chivalry was sportsmanship.

The hardening of the idea of courtesy and the rise of the concept of chivalry were mirrored clearly when at last the two greatest champions of East and West faced each

ABOVE AND BELOW: *In the Steps of the Crusaders.* COURTESY HASTINGS HOUSE AND LIBRARIE HACHETTE

THE MIGHTIEST CRUSADER CASTLE

Of all the crusader castles the strongest and best preserved is the Krak of the Chevaliers. This Hospitaller stronghold, which was completed during the Third Crusade, served to guard Palestine's northern approaches. The view below shows its plan. There are two concentric walls, each dominated by several round towers. Between the walls was a lake-sized moat that was also the fortress's reservoir. Within the inner walls is the chapel (below left) with its pointed arches similar to windows in European churches of that time. Above the chapel is the site of a round table for the knights' conferences (stone circle in the photograph at the left). The castle stayed in crusader hands for 161 years, until Sultan Baibars took it in 1271.

AEROFILM, LTD.

cordiam fuam: 7 i

pud me oratio

cam deo fusceptor

Although the Third Crusade was a large-scale war, it was also a personal tilting match between Richard and

ecte canticū eius.

eo uite mee : di

neis es.

PERMISSION OF THE TRUSTEES OF THE BRITISH MUSEUM

Saladin. In this beautiful illuminated manuscript Saladin is shown (above right) being unhorsed by Richard.

LANDESBIBLIOTHEQUE, FULDA

MINISTRY OF WORKS, CROWN COPYRIGHT RESERVED

other. Their meeting was, in a way, symbolic of the strength and weakness of both worlds. These two champions were Saladin and King Richard I of England, called the Lion-Heart.

Richard, whose great-great-grandfather was William the Conqueror, had sworn to go on crusade in 1187 when the woeful news of the fall of Jerusalem had reached Europe. That news had plunged all Christendom into mourning. Frederick Barbarossa, the Holy Roman emperor, had sworn to go to Palestine; King Philip of France had taken the cross as well, along with many other barons and lords.

Immediately after his coronation in 1189, Richard, knowing he must have plenty of treasure if he was to pay an army large enough to retake the Holy Land, began to look for sources of revenue. "I would sell London if I could find a buyer," he is reported to have exclaimed. By July of 1190 he had settled all his affairs, had stripped his realm of all the gold he could acquire, and was ready to start on crusade.

It was high time, for there were grim tidings from the

BIBLIOTHEQUE NATIONALE

In front of the British Parliament buildings in London stands a heroic statue of Richard (left). His fellow leaders on the Third Crusade were Emperor Frederick Barbarossa of the Holy Roman Empire and King Philip II of France. Frederick, shown with his sons at far left, drowned on the way to the Holy Land. Philip, shown at right with Richard, was the Lion-Heart's constant rival.

East. All the cities once held by the Franks, except for Tyre and Tripoli, were in the hands of Saladin. The Franks had besieged the important city of Acre in the hope of retaking it, but had been surrounded in turn by Saladin's army and were being slowly starved. Worse yet, Emperor Frederick Barbarossa, who had gone to Asia with a large German army, had drowned while crossing a river in northern Syria; without his leadership his men had begun to desert, and only a relatively small number finally reached Acre. There they joined the other crusaders.

King Richard had arranged to go with King Philip of France. The two monarchs set out together on July 4, 1190. But there was to be almost a full year of delay before the Lion-Heart could reach Acre.

Traveling by different routes, the two kings met again at Messina, in Sicily, where they were to rest and provision their armies. Here, proud Richard was insulted by the inhabitants, so he invaded the city, captured it, and planted his banner on its walls. But peace was made at last and the kings wintered there. In the spring Philip sailed to Tyre and went on from there to Acre.

After taking the time to subjugate the strategically and financially valuable island of Cyprus, Richard finally arrived at Acre in June, 1191. Now, with his fresh forces and those of the French king's, which had arrived somewhat earlier, the assault on Acre grew hotter. King Philip had built some excellent siege engines, including a catapult called the Bad Neighbor and a scaling ladder known as the Cat because it clung to walls when it was put against them. Richard too had built several catapults and two trebuchets, or great slings, one of which killed twelve men with a single huge stone. One attack followed another, and there was bloody fighting on the walls and towers. Finally, worn out and starving, the city surrendered.

The French king, who had been ill almost all of the time, now decided to return home, where certain problems of state waited for him. When he left, Richard took command of the Crusade. He began to negotiate with Saladin over the ransom for the Saracens taken prisoner at Acre.

Saladin had been having his own troubles with his princes, some of whom were becoming weary of the war. He had not wanted Acre to surrender, but he could not gather enough men to make a massive strike for its safety. He himself was feeling the weight of the many years of fighting, and he was suffering from illness. He agreed to pay a huge sum of money, to return the True Cross, and to release a number of Christian prisoners. He paid the first installment of the money and sent back some of his prisoners, but he did not altogether trust the Franks. During the haggling that followed, Richard cold-bloodedly ordered that the twenty-six hundred Saracen prisoners he held be executed. He explained that he had done it because Saladin had not kept his part of the bargain. His chroniclers said that the Franks thanked God for this chance to avenge their friends who had died during the siege. But it was an act difficult to apologize for, and one that made the war even more bitter.

Richard now left Acre and began to march toward Jerusalem. As usual, the Saracens hung about the edges of the Frankish columns, picking off stragglers. Saladin mean-

ISRAEL GOVERNMENT TOURIST OFFICE

The seawall of Acre

When the crusaders had to overcome high-walled cities, such as Acre, that blocked their way to Jerusalem, they pitched their tents and began the furious siege. But life in their camp and within the besieged city went on as best it could beyond the battle's din. The painter of this miniature thus shows not only the warriors at work (middle section) but also horses being cared for inside the walls (top) and a calm game of chess in the tents (bottom).

IBLIOTHÈQUE NATIONALE. SERVICE PHOTOGRAPHIQUE

while had set his host in hiding in a forest just north of the town of Arsuf. The forest bordered an open plain that stretched some two miles to the sea. On September 7, 1191, as the Franks were marching through the plain on their way to the key city of Jaffa, the Moslems burst from their cover and fell upon them.

Richard had long since prepared for any attack. He was a far better general than any crusader before him had been, and he knew how to use his infantry—especially his archers. During the last hundred years the hand crossbow, or arbalest, had been developed out of the siege engine called the ballista, which was itself a giant crossbow. Using the arbalest and shooting short, heavy arrows called bolts, or quarrels, the Franks had a range almost as great as that of the Turks with their powerful shortbows. Richard formed his bowmen into long lines facing the enemy, and behind them he placed his knights. Too many crusaders had been lost in previous campaigns by impetuously charging out after the swift and lightly armored Saracens. Richard gave the strict command that his men must stand fast in their ranks until he blew the trumpets for the charge.

The crossbowmen returned the enemy's fire with deadly effect. Richard rode up and down the lines encouraging his men and waiting for the Saracens to come closer. Just as he was about to signal the charge, some of the Hospitallers, no longer able to bear being shot at without fighting back, raised their war cry and dashed out against the Saracens. Richard ordered the trumpets to sound, and he himself cantered forward.

Saladin's men were pressed close together and could not withstand the Christians' charge. They broke and ran, and were butchered in their tracks.

Richard gathered his men and charged again, and then a third time. The Turkish troops were smashed and routed. Seven hundred men fell on the Christian side, but their loss had achieved its purpose.

The Sultan retreated toward Jerusalem while Richard moved to Jaffa where his men could rest and enjoy the green gardens, the abundant food, and the pleasures of the town. The King knew he would have to return home soon, and he began negotiating a truce with Saladin. The negotiations dragged on until November, with great shows of chivalry and courtesy on both sides.

And then, despite such desperately gallant gestures as Richard's offer to give his sister in marriage to Saladin's brother, the negotiations collapsed. With the beginning

AVIO CASTELLO, FOTO RENZI

Richard recruited Italian archers to supplement his infantry's ranks.

Richard was both charming and cruel, chivalrous and treacherous. He and Saladin's emissaries had many cordial meetings, which may have looked like the regal scene below. But he was also capable of such uncivil acts as the massacre of his Saracen hostages (left).

BOTH: BIBLIOTHEQUE NATIONALE, SERVICE PHOTOGRAPHIQUE

of the heavy November rains, Saladin disbanded half his army and went into winter quarters at Jerusalem.

The weather grew worse, but Richard decided to try to reach the Holy City. He took his army to Ramleh, and then soon after Christmas, 1191, on into the hills of Judea. By January 3 they were within a dozen miles of Jerusalem and had met nothing but slight resistance from small parties of Saracens.

But the weather was more deadly than the enemy. A cold rain poured down, turning the land to mud. A freezing wind tore up the tent pegs and blew down the tents. The crusaders' stores of food were ruined by the torrent; their armor, which they had polished by rolling in barrels of sand in preparation for the glorious adventure, was rusty and muddy. If they had only known it, Saladin's men in Jerusalem were suffering too from cold and wet. But Richard's advisers, the barons who had lived in the Holy Land all their lives and who had ruined the Second Crusade, persuaded the King to turn back. Even if he could get to Jerusalem through the mud and wet, and even if he could take the city—which was doubtful, since reinforcements had come to Saladin from Egypt—how could he hold it? His own men would want to go home, and there would not be enough soldiers among the native forces to guard the city against the armies of the Sultan. Richard gave in. He returned to Ramleh and then to Ascalon where he strengthened the fortress walls and waited out the winter.

The French troops remaining from Philip's expedition were beginning to desert, and Richard's treasury was running low. There was the usual discord among the crusaders; the usual quarreling over who would rule the land when Richard left. And to make matters worse, news came from England that the King's brother John was taking the kingdom into his own hands. It was clear that now a truce would have to be made with Saladin, if only to allow Richard to leave for home.

It is difficult for us to understand the events of this period except in the contradictory terms of chivalry. Both sides wanted peace; each respected and even admired the other. Yet the hatred between Christian and infidel was strong, and even stronger were the desires to free the land where Christ had lived and, like true knights, to perform deeds of high courage. On the Friday before Palm Sunday, 1192, a band of young knights raided the Saracen territory and captured some cattle, killing thirty Moslems and taking fifty more prisoner. On Palm Sunday itself,

BODLEIAN LIBRARY, OXFORD

As the illustrations from this 14th-century manuscript show, siege warfare had changed very little two centuries after Richard's Crusade. The knights still had to penetrate the walls of the fortress either by undermining them (see soldiers swinging picks, above) or by battering their way in. Once the knights were within the fortress there came the brutal hand-to-hand combat that the artist depicts with such realism. But Richard's soldiers did not have the visors and plate armor leggings that these knights are wearing.

Saladin's nephew arrived at Ascalon; there, in a splendid ceremony, King Richard girded the young Saracen with the belt of knighthood. In July Saladin attacked Jaffa and took it. Richard at once set out to its rescue. Sailing his galleys into the harbor, he leaped into the water and led his men ashore. In a swift, wild attack, the King recaptured the city. The very next morning peace talks began again as the Lion-Heart breakfasted and jested with the Saracen princes he had captured.

Richard had with him only fifty-four knights and about two thousand infantrymen, many of them crossbowmen. Saladin tried one more desperate bid to finish off the King. At dawn on August 5 the alarm was raised in the Christian camp. A force of more than seven thousand Moslem horsemen was swooping down on them.

Richard pulled on his coat of mail and at once arrayed his men according to his new tactical plan. He set a front line of infantry, kneeling behind their shields with their spears leveled. Behind the infantry were the crossbowmen in two ranks, the first rank shooting, the second reloading the weapons. The Turks charged in wave after wave but were turned back from the bristling hedge of spearpoints; and since they wore almost no armor, they were badly punished by the deadly, continuous rain of crossbow bolts. As they milled about in confusion, the infantry opened its ranks and the King charged out with his handful of knights, only fifteen of them on horseback. With the standard of the lion floating behind him, Richard seemed to be everywhere. The Earl of Leicester was unhorsed. The Lion-Heart spurred to his side and defended him while he remounted. A knight named Ralph of Mauleon was seized by several Turks, and the King cantered up and freed him. Then occurred one of those incidents which illustrate better than anything else the courtesy of both sides. Richard's horse was killed under him and he was fighting on foot. A Moslem galloped up with two fine steeds and said they had been sent by Saladin himself. The King remounted with thanks and rewarded the messenger.

The crusaders hoped that either by treaty or by conquest they could gain access to the holy places of Jerusalem. In the words of the Middle Ages they would then "put the finishing touch to virtue by adoring Christ in the very place where the gospel first shone forth from the cross." The large domed structure in the walled Jerusalem of this 15th-century miniature is the Dome of the Rock; the cluster of domes at upper left is the Holy Sepulchre. Coming into the city are pilgrims of high and low degree.

BIBLIOTHÈQUE NATIONALE, SERVICE PHOTOGRAPHIQUE

NATIONALBIBLIOTHEK, VIENNA

*Tambourines and stringed instru-
ments set the tone of Moslem courts
(left), luxurious but cultivated.
Based on the Koran, the Moslems'
rights and obligations were passed
on from father to son (below).*

BIBLIOTHEQUE NATIONALE, SERVICE PHOTOGRAPHIQUE

BURGERBIBLIOTHEK, BERN

Richard, never a good sailor, took a land route home. To avoid his enemies he disguised himself as a woodsman. But it was not in his character to act a humble part, and he was soon recognized (above).

By evening this final battle was over, and hundreds of the enemy lay dead. A month later a five-year treaty of peace was signed between Richard and Saladin. By its terms the cities along the coast as far south as Jaffa were left to the crusaders, but Ascalon, which was too close to Jerusalem for comfort, was to be leveled. Christians and Moslems were allowed to pass through each other's lands, and pilgrims were permitted to visit the shrines of the Holy Land. Richard was ill when the pact was signed, but he sent to Saladin to tell him, courteously, that after the truce was over he would return with men to rescue all of Palestine if Saladin would face him in the field. Saladin replied that he had such a high opinion of the Lion-Heart's honor and excellence that, by Allah, if he had to lose his lands he would rather lose them to Richard than any other.

King Richard's adventure, the Third Crusade, was over, and soon afterward the two great champions met their ends as well. Saladin, ailing and exhausted, came down with a fatal fever in 1193, at the age of fifty-five. He died patiently and with a smile while hearing a reading from the Koran, the Bible of the Mohammedans. As for King Richard, he started home in the autumn of 1192, but as he attempted to cross through Austria he was recognized and imprisoned by the soldiers of a fellow crusader and an old enemy, Duke Leopold of Austria. Leopold had never forgotten that his banner had been removed by Richard from the towers of Acre when both had captured the city a year before. It was not until March, 1194, that he was finally released on the payment of a large ransom. Five years later, while fighting against one of his own vassals in France, the Lion-Heart was killed by a stray arrow.

85

UNIVERSITATSBIBLIOTHEK, HEIDELBEE

VI TO BE A KNIGHT

The peace that Richard and Saladin forged with such valor in 1192 lasted long after they had left the scene. But it was preserved, in various forms, more because of weaknesses on both sides than because of strength and determination. It endured, and both in the crusader states and in Europe knighthood was allowed to flower into new forms of nobility. The rather primitive oath of feudal homage and the early hopes of the Church for a morally better man had, surprisingly, borne fruit. Within the course of a hundred embattled years knighthood had developed into a kind of fraternity, not merely military but deeply religious and social as well.

To become a knight was no longer a simple matter. Chivalry itself was now practically a religious order, with its own rules, its own rituals, and its own special codes of behavior. Not every knight lived up to the high standard required of him, of course; the important thing was that the high standard now existed by which a knight could be judged for his nobility rather than for his ruthlessness.

"The common people spoil their children," says a thirteenth-century sermon, "and make them little red frocks, and then when they are older set them to the plough. But nobles first set their children beneath them and make them eat with the serving lads, and then when they are grown up set them on high." To be a knight required that you start young, for you had many things to learn, not simply about warfare but about courtesy as well.

The son of a knight might be taken from the care of his mother as early as seven years of age and sent off to the castle of some powerful nobleman to begin his training as a page. Every kind of menial job was his: fetching and

THE PIERPONT MORGAN LIBRARY

The heroes of a new age were courtly knights, like this flower-bedecked rider (left) on his way to see his lady. But with all their mannered graces, they did not forget their virtues of strength and piety; and for all their elegant trappings, knights still had to fight and to struggle into armor (above).

BOTH: *The Color of Chivalry*, IMPERIAL CHEMICAL INDUSTRIES

Battle dress continued to be efficient, but considerably more decorative.

carrying, running errands, helping the lady of the household in all her many duties, learning to come when he was called and to wait patiently when there was nothing for him to do. As he grew older, his day filled. He might be taught to play some musical instrument, to compose verse, to wait on table, to curry horses and care for hawks. He learned the use of arms—the sword, the lance, the axe, on which his life would someday depend—and he practiced wrestling, leaping, running, and vaulting into the saddle without touching the stirrup while in full armor. All this training prepared him for the next step: to become a squire, at about the age of fourteen.

And now there were still other details of service to learn and perform. As a squire he had to know how to carve every sort of meat at the table and to know the correct word for each type of carving. A deer was *broken*, a swan was *lifted*, a hen was *despoiled*, a duck was *unbraced*, and a peacock was *disfigured*. He had to know every aspect of the hunt, with the right words to describe a *skulk* of foxes, a *sounder* of swine, or a *pride* of lions; he had to be familiar with the care and repairing of armor, with the management of hounds, with the mews where the hawks were manned and trained. As squire of the bedchamber he must help his lord undress, comb his hair, prepare his bed, and even "drive out the dog and the cat, giving them a clout." As squire of the body he must keep his lord's weapons and armor in good condition, replacing worn leather and burnishing away rust; as squire of the stables he must groom and exercise horses and learn how to train a war-horse so that it would stand still if its master was unseated in battle, or move or halt at the single word of command; as squire of the table he must cut bread, pour wine, and serve properly with a napkin over his arm.

But in all these tasks it was never forgotten that he was not just a servant. He was an apprentice, preparing to take his place in the order of knighthood. Much more than bodily fitness and a readiness to serve were thus required of the young man who would be a knight. He had to learn manners and attitudes and above all, the meaning of honor.

Honor had grown out of the military and feudal side of knighthood. Virtue, which had come from knighthood's religious wellsprings, was equally important for the would-be knight—as the priests never tired of repeating. Ramón Lull, who was first a knight at the Spanish court and then a missionary to the Saracens, wrote in his *Book of the Order of Chivalry* that a knight should show moderation in all things, that he should avoid laziness, envy, and haughtiness. He condemns those knights who are "proud of their beauty of fashion . . . who hold the mirror in the hand . . . and other jollities." Certainly the profound religious feeling, which was as much a part of the Crusades as the desire to win lands and wealth, helped instill some of these Christian virtues into young nobles.

But there were courtly virtues, too, which brought manners into being. These expressed themselves chiefly in the changing attitude toward women.

There were many reasons for the change. Youngsters taken from their mothers and sent away to another home where they had to work hard would naturally associate the idea of Mother with the happy, carefree days of childhood. Their new tasks were often to help the ladies of the castle, and they might in return be treated with the gentleness due a small boy far from home. It is to be expected that they would be taught by their new friends to be gentle and affectionate where women were concerned. Many knights made the Virgin Mary their special patroness, instead of the more warlike saints.

The Crusades brought the knights of the south, of Provence and Italy, together with the rougher soldiers of northern France, Germany, and England. The men of the north, it was said, loved battle, but the southerners loved life. It was inevitable that some of this love of life—of milder pleasures, of love, of parties and dances and games— would rub off onto the northerners. Besides, the Crusades brought more wealth into Europe, more luxuries, a greater desire for comfort. The new castle, built of stone, carpeted and hung with tapestries or embroideries to keep out the chill, was now as much a court as it was a farm or fortress. Even the songs reflected the change. Where once the minstrels had sung only of war, of the slashing off of heads and the breaking of bones, they now borrowed from the troubadours of the south songs of love, of sacrifice, and of tenderness.

No one is quite sure just how the troubadours developed or what some of their songs really meant. It is believed by some historians that they may have been members of a secret cult, a kind of brotherhood with its own passwords and hidden symbols. Most of them were nobles, some were commoners, but they all held to the same complicated rules of composition, rhyme, and structure, and they all spoke mysteriously of "domnei"—the power a certain unknown Lady had over them. Some sang their own songs and poems

UNIVERSITATSBIBLIOTHEK, HEIDELBERG

Knights were dressed and equipped by their pages. Then, recognizable only by their peculiar caparisons, they rode off to the tournament.

UNIVERSITATSBIBLIOTHEK, HEIDELBERG

THE PIERPONT MORGAN LIBRARY

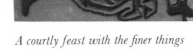

Time for falconry

A courtly feast with the finer things

PHOTO BY ARCHIVIO DI STATO, PISA

A medieval court of justice

THE COURTLY KNIGHT

The castle of the European noble was no longer the drafty barn that it once had been. Ladies and knights of the court now dined in a sumptuous hall at a table set with plates and serving dishes and were waited on by solicitous servants (left). There was more wealth, greater security, and more leisure. In this atmosphere outdoor sports were developed, the most popular of which was the tournament; and indoor games like Persian "shah," or chess, were played to pass away the hours. A wider spread of learning also contributed to the changing pattern of the knight's life. He no longer had to rely on the priests of the Church to write his letters and business communications; either he was sufficiently versed in Latin to do it himself or he could handle the matter in the local language. But along with this increasingly rich and secular life went a greater awareness of the difference between those who were noble and those who were not. Knighthood became more and more an exclusive mark of privilege, and those most conscious of their nobility were the men who had just been knighted.

BIBLIOTECA DEL MONASTERIO DE EL ESCORIAL, MADRID

The ladies and a page dressed for chess

as they traveled from castle to castle; others were accompanied by *jongleurs*, or singers, with better voices than their own. They sang of knights whose first desires were to please their ladies, about ladies who were the inspiration for gallant deeds. Bernard of Ventadour, one of the greatest of them, said, "To sing is worth nothing if the song does not come from the heart. And the song cannot come from the heart if there is no delicate and profound love there."

It must not be thought that the ladies of this time were soft, languishing doves or lily-handed, fairy-tale princesses. They could inherit property and be feudal landholders themselves, and they knew how to defend their property. They were brought up to ride, to hunt, to use certain weapons, to command as their husbands and fathers did, and when their men went off to a crusade without them, they were quite capable of managing the estate and protecting it alone. Some of them, like Countess Blanche of Champagne, did not hesitate to put on armor and lead their troops to war. And in peacetime they had to act as overseers for farmland and castle, manage a retinue of servants and retainers, see to the cooking, the making of clothes, the spinning and weaving—the hundreds of tasks necessary in the management of a large estate. They were, on the whole, tough and capable wives for warlike husbands, with hands as hard and calloused as any man's.

Still, they too changed under the influence of the age. Their dress became more elaborate, so that the priests cried out in horror against these vain peacocks. They discovered silks and gold tissue, rouge and perfume; they made their chambers prettier with gilding and painting; they planted sweet herbs and flowers in their gardens; they cultivated music and poetry, and fourteen of them are known to have been famous troubadours in their own right.

The young squire not only swore to defend womankind but he chose a lady whose token he wore and to whom he vowed to be faithful. When at last he received his weapons and was allowed to fight in tournaments, it was under the eye of his lady that he fought, and for her glory.

The tournament was the most popular of games and was a kind of high point in the career of the young man aiming for his spurs and belt. In it can be seen all the aspects of chivalry: elaborate ritual and fine show, courage, honor, championship of ladies, and knightly virtue. Only the Church rather crankily insisted that those who wasted their time on tournaments would go to hell.

DRAWING AFTER MATTHEW PARIS *Chronicles*

The surcoat this knight wears over his mail shirt is marked with crosses. Hands are protected by mittens at the end of mailed sleeves.

BIBLIOTHEQUE NATIONALE, PHOTO BY GIRAUDON

When a tourney was given, it was often used as the occasion for the arming of a group of young squires or for the bestowing of knighthood. It might represent, then, the maiden bow of a young man in the world of arms through his appearance in a mock battle, where it could be seen whether he displayed the proper courage and bearing. The twelfth-century chronicler Roger of Hoveden said:

A knight cannot shine in war if he has not prepared for it in tournaments. He must have seen his own blood flow, have had his teeth crackle under the blow of his adversary, have been dashed to earth with such force as to feel the weight of his foe, and disarmed twenty times; he must twenty times have retrieved his failures, more set than ever upon the combat. Then he will be able to confront actual war with the hope of being victorious.

A day or two before the tournament the ceremonies would be held, either bestowing swords upon young squires who were not yet to become knights but could now fight in battles or giving the accolade of knighthood to those who were ready for it. The candidates for knighthood were bathed and then dressed in white robes. With their armor and swords on the altar of the chapel, they spent the night

Despite the new emphasis on nobility, successful warriors were still knighted by other knights on the field of battle with the colée.

ALL: UNIVERSITÄTSBIBLIOTHEK, HEIDELBERG

in prayer. The following morning they were led into church by older knights who acted as their sponsors; here they heard a sermon in which they were instructed to devote their lives to the service of God and of chivalry. Then, dressed in the *vair and gris*—the patterned furs of knighthood—they were brought before the nobleman who was to give them their rank. He would say, "Be worthy!" and strike the blow of the *colée*. Their sponsors would fix on their spurs and gird them with their belt and sword.

This ceremony varied from place to place. In some cases the *colée* was not given. Often a man would be knighted on the field of war with no ceremony other than the *colée* and the receiving of his belt and sword. Although there are mentions of priests performing the ceremony, it was generally felt that only a knight could give knighthood to another. Still later in history it was held that only the king or his representatives, the great barons, could invest a man with noble rank.

The tournament then might last several days, and each evening would be full of dancing and feasting—at any rate for those who could still walk and had teeth enough left to chew with. It was usually divided into two types of event: the joust, or duel with lances between two horsemen; and the melee, or sham battle between two companies of knights. The account of one such fine tournament was written by the troubadour Jacques Bretel in 1285. Although this is a good deal later than the period we have been speaking of, its description fits closely enough.

It was given at Chauvency, in northern France, by the Count of Chiny, and many noblemen came to take part in it. The nearby villages and towns were packed with visitors, and booths were set up in the marketplaces, selling all sorts of goods. There were minstrels and jugglers and musicians and dancers, and the racket and excitement must have been staggering. A place was staked out in a large open field for the lists, which were two wooden fences, one inside the other, making a protected area in which the knights fought.

On Monday morning, when the galleries, or wooden

Virtues and vices were constantly preached for the edification of the new nobility. A manuscript miniaturist named Honoré painted some of these qualities. At right: humility, pride taking a fall, the humble sinner at confession, and hypocrisy. Knights were also counseled to be generous to women. They did so by winning their favor in tournaments (top left), in singing and musical contests (bottom), and by defending them in battle. The women occasionally repaid this kindness by dropping rocks on the enemy (center).

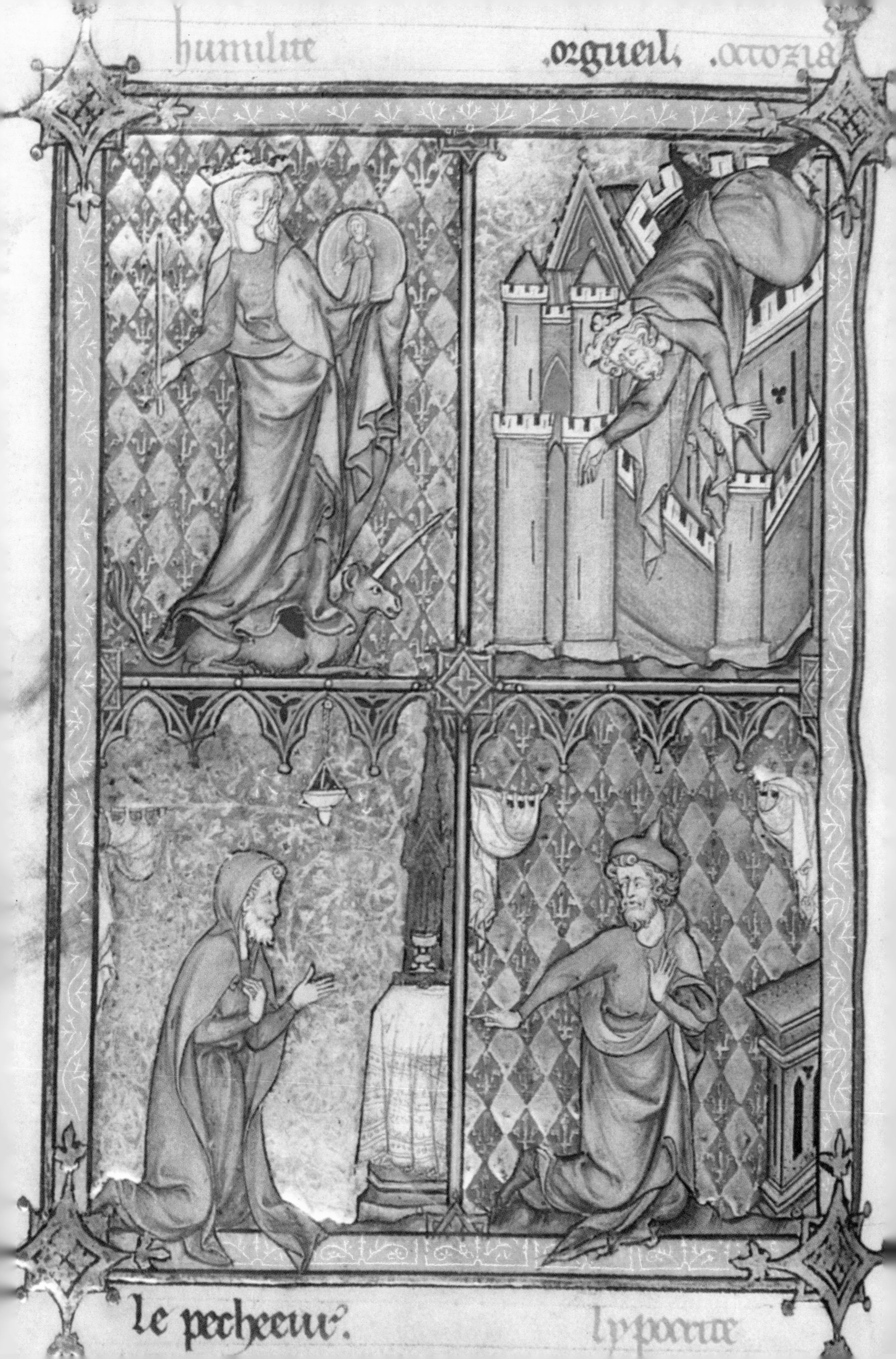
humilite
orgueil
ocozia
le pecheeur.
ypocrite

bleachers, were filled with ladies and gentlemen, and when the countryfolk had crowded up as close as they could in the meadow, the first jousts were held. It is noteworthy that on the day before, the names and crests of all those who were to fight had been displayed, and any contestant who was accused of being discourteous or unworthy was refused permission to appear.

"Ferri of Chardogne leaped into the saddle," says Jacques Bretel, "his shield covering him, his helm laced [that is, tied under his chin with thongs], his lance in his fist, and trotted out so hardily that all the earth trembled." He met the Lord of Bazentin and was thrown from his horse with a broken arm. Jousters held their spears pointing to the left side. The object was to strike one's opponent on the shield or helmet so that one's own lance flew to pieces and the other man was unhorsed. To touch a man anywhere below his sword-belt was counted a foul, and we still use the expression "hitting below the belt." Lances usually had flat or blunted heads in these duels of pleasure, and were made of light wood that would splinter easily. Sometimes, flying splinters could cause more damage than the blow of the lance itself.

Seven jousts, or tilts as they were called, were held on the first day at Chauvency, and ten on the second. On Thursday the melee for which everyone was waiting was held between a company of knights called the challengers and another group called the challenged. They were armed with blunted swords or with maces. Entering the lists, both sides were drawn up in order with a rope separating them. All about the enclosure marshals and heralds were stationed to see that order was kept and the rules observed and to judge the conduct of the fighters. At the command, "Let

The joust, or single-pair combat, was fought according to formal rules. The knights usually fought in this agreed pattern: mounted combat with lances

them go!'' the rope was cut and both sides charged.

On every hand, says Bretel, war cries rang out. Amid clouds of dust could be seen the colorful patterns painted on shields and the gleam of armor. Henri of Blâmont was surrounded by opponents, and two of his friends rushed to his rescue and drove them off. Joffroi of Aspremont, with one stroke of his sword, split the helm of the Lord of Bergues, broke its laces, and beat it from his head. Great blows were exchanged, the ladies applauded, and the heralds shouted encouragement.

At last, darkness fell. The chief marshal threw down his staff and ended the tournament. That night a great banquet was held where prizes were given to those who were judged to have borne themselves best. Bretel himself was asked to recite some of his poems, and so delightful was the evening, says he, that Friday came all too soon.

It is thought that some aspects of this rather rough sport may have been learned from the Saracens. If so, it would be only one more item in a long list of borrowings from all parts of the Arab world; a list which includes our present number system (with the marvelous invention of zero), a good deal of medical knowledge, much scholarship—including the theory that the earth is round—many fruits and vegetables, sugar cane and cotton, paper and new kinds of cloth, many scientific devices, new methods of working leather and steel and clay—the list is almost endless.

Another important addition to chivalry which may possibly have come from the Saracens was the heraldic badge, or blazon. Certainly it began to be widely used during the Crusades and especially after the introduction of the closed helmet, which prevented a man's face being seen. Distinctive designs were painted on the shield so that

BIBLIOTHÈQUE NATIONALE, SERVICE PHOTOGRAPHIQUE

(which sometimes had sharpened points, but were always aimed at the shielded body), followed by a duel on foot, then surrender on bended knee.

97

The melee, as witnessed in this colorful 15th-century painting, began at a signal from the referee. The knights

scrimmaged bravely beneath the admiring glances of the ladies, while the pages made off for safety (right).

PERMISSION OF THE TRUSTEES OF THE BRITISH MUSEUM

the knight could be recognized, and in later times these designs were sewn on his surcoat and the trappings of his horse. Beginning as a personal badge, they became by degrees hereditary badges to be handed down in his family; a man who bore such a blazon on his shield could be known not only for *who* he was but for *what* he was as well—a member of the knightly caste.

The man, then, who had gone through the long training process, who had been armed in a solemn ritual, who was familiar with the use of weapons and had practiced them in the tournament, who had taken the knightly oaths and wore a heraldic device, who held lands and castles and passed them and the family crest and war cry on to his son, was, by the year 1200, very conscious of the difference between himself and the rest of society. He had become an aristocrat, a man who thought that his very blood was unlike that of the common people.

Among the Saxons who formed the shield-wall at Senlac field there were, of course, distinctions between serfs and free men, between those who held much land and those who held little, between leaders and followers, and between powerful fighters and lesser ones. But among the Normans the distinctions were much sharper. There were definite gradations between mounted men and those who fought on foot, between rich landholders and poor adventurers who hoped to become landholders, between overlords and their vassals and *their* hired soldiers. But now the line was drawn everywhere in Europe. There was an immobile, aristocratic structure that pigeonholed a man forever. In spite of their wealth, strength, leadership, or power, a strict barrier separated those who were brothers-in-arms in the noble fraternity from those who were not.

The increase in luxury helped to make the difference more obvious. Many knights, particularly those who had had some contact with the East, wanted to live as befitted their rank. And to supply their brocades and silks, their pearls, their spices and sugar, their Damascus sword blades and Persian carpets, a quite unfeudal and unaristocratic sort of activity was needed—trade. Trade and those who made it were to play an important and fatal role in the history of the Crusades.

Despite precautions taken by the knights and their armorers, there were fractured limbs and broken heads in tournaments. The ladies at right gasp as one rider pierces his opponent's helmet and unhorses him. Some knights, like the flag bearer above, made the Virgin Mary their patroness.

VERSITATSBIBLIOTHEK, HEIDELBERG

VII SACK OF CONSTANTINOPLE

The fourth, and most tragic, of the six great Crusades began at a tournament in northern France in an atmosphere of nobility and luxury.

A new military venture into the East had been in the air for a long time. The results of the Third Crusade had been meager. At the end of the twelfth century the Franks held only Tripoli, Antioch, and a narrow strip of coast stretching for ninety miles from Jaffa to Tyre. Jerusalem, that city whose recovery had been the object of the Third Crusade, was still in Moslem hands. And the interminable rivalries among the barons of the Eastern kingdom continued as before. When Innocent III had become pope in 1198, he spoke of his deep desire to send an army to the Holy Land. The year before that, Henry VI, the Holy Roman emperor, had planned a crusade that was cut short by his sudden death. By 1199 two of Pope Innocent's representatives were preaching the holy war. One of them, Cardinal Peter of Capua, proclaimed that all who took the cross would be given full pardon for their sins. The other, an itinerant priest named Fulk of Neuilly, was even more dramatic. His preaching, so men thought, was accompanied by heavenly signs and miracles.

In November, 1199, Count Thibaut of Champagne held a tourney. Many knights came to joust and to ride in the melee, and on the day following the sport, the Count invited Fulk to give a sermon. The Crusade must have been preached with more than usual fervor, for not only did Count Thibaut and his cousin Count Louis of Blois take the cross but all his guests did so too. During the next few months the movement spread rapidly, and hundreds of other noblemen swore to join.

MONASTERY OF SAN BENEDICT, SUBIACO. PHOTO BY ALINARI

The Greek soldier at left is shown standing in awe at the foot of the cross of Christ. This exquisite mosaic is an example of the sumptuous art of Constantinople, capital of the Byzantine Empire and focus of the tragic Fourth Crusade. The Crusade was preached by Pope Innocent III (at right).

Another who attended the famous tournament and took the cross was Geoffrey of Villehardouin, Marshal of Champagne. Because of his knightly honor and tact, Villehardouin was deemed one of the best possible ambassadors when it came to the delicate business of transporting the eager crusaders to the East.

Since Byzantium was no longer powerful enough to furnish them with help for the land route, they would go by sea. Venice had the greatest fleet on the seas; accordingly, early in 1201, Geoffrey of Villehardouin and five other envoys were sent to negotiate with the Venetians for transportation.

Venice was a city full of mystery but based solidly on business. It had grown rich from trade with the cloth and wine centers in western and northern Europe. Its ambitious and powerful merchant families financed navies that sailed everywhere in the Mediterranean, doing business with Saracen and Frank alike.

At the time of Villehardouin's visit, the leader, or doge, of the republic of Venice was Enrico Dandolo, a very old man and partly blind but full of vigor and ambition, a worthy chief of a shrewd commercial city. The Doge and his council agreed to furnish ships and provisions for the crusaders at a price of 85,000 marks. He also seemed to agree to their decision to attack Egypt first, since that was where Moslem power was then centered. And also "for the love of God," as he smoothly put it, the Venetians would add fifty armed galleys to the fleet for the assault on Egypt. Of course, there would be a small price for these as well: merely that Venice receive half of all conquests of land or money.

This arrangement was at length ratified by the people of the city when ten thousand of them assembled in and around the Church of St. Mark. It was a touching moment as they shouted, "We consent, we consent!"

Yet, unknown to Villehardouin and the Venetian citizens, representatives of the Doge were at that moment in Egypt. They were there to negotiate a trade agreement with the sultan and to promise him that Venice would never carry a war into his lands. Much more desirable in Venetian eyes than a ruinous crusade was an expedition to Constanti-

COIN GALLERIES, INC. N.Y.

Money in the form of both Venetian and crusader coins (above) had much to do with the Fourth Crusade. More and more currencies were needed as Europe lost its insularity and as traders spread out across the Mediterranean. At right merchants are seen surviving a storm en route to the Holy Land.

BIBLIOTECA DEL MONASTERIO DE EL ESCORIAL, MADRID

Como un mercador ya en sa naue a altr roue gn tormenta

E prometeu sa offerta bõa a S. M. de salas t tormenta qdou logo

Como chegaron a altr t foron mui leti p en

Como uenden mui ben todas sas mercadurias q̃ trey

Como se tornar a sa terra sãos t con saure t con grãança

Como compriro sa romaria a salas t deron y sas offertas

nople where the new emperor, Alexius III, was balking at signing a trade agreement. As it happened, Constantinople was also much in the mind of the new leader of the Fourth Crusade—the man who had been elected upon the death of Count Thibaut. He was Boniface, Marquis of Montferrat, a wealthy and valiant knight who had fought against Saladin. Boniface had become friendly with the younger Alexius, the nephew of the new emperor and the son of the former emperor, Isaac II, who had been deposed and imprisoned. Because of that friendship and the knowledge that a cooperative emperor would help the Crusade, it is very likely that during the winter of 1201–2 plans were made to take the crusading army to Egypt by way of Constantinople. If such plans were made, no one was told about them. Villehardouin does not mention them. Publicly, at least, the aim of Montferrat's expedition remained the attack on Egypt.

Would-be crusaders then began arriving in Venice in considerable numbers (around 30,000). The Venetians lodged them on an island where they could camp without

GUSTAVE DORE

The magnificent Church of St. Mark in Venice (right) still stands as evidence of the Venetians' love for richness and color. Merchant-sailors of the city ranged across the Mediterranean, returning with treasures from Byzantium and other lands to gild the elaborate façade and vaulted interior spaces of their church. It was within St. Mark's that the doge, or leader, of Venice pledged himself to join the Fourth Crusade. The 19th-century artist Gustave Doré included angels in that scene, at left.

too much crowding, and then demanded that they pay the promised fee of 85,000 pieces of silver before any ships were provided. Even though some of the chiefs borrowed money and contributed their own silver and gold plates and cups, the army could scrape together no more than 51,000 silver marks. It looked as though the Crusade was at an end before it had begun. At this moment the Doge came forward with another proposition.

Across the Adriatic Sea, on the coast of Dalmatia, lay the strong port city of Zara, which Venice claimed. The king of Hungary now held it. If the crusaders would help take the city and restore it to Venetian control, the debt of 34,000 marks would be suspended—not canceled—until it could be paid out of further conquests. Boniface of Montferrat and most of the other nobles agreed to this.

In November, 1202, the fleet sailed for Zara. Montferrat remained behind in Venice "for some business that detained him." But the other great barons went with the host, along with more than three hundred siege engines and a great many Venetians, led by the Doge himself.

PHOTO BY SCALA

PALAZZO DUCALE, VENICE, PHOTO BY ALINARI

The destruction of Zara was undoubtedly as gory and confused a spectacle as Tintoretto showed it in his painting, above, with arrows and crossbow bolts arching through the sky above the incoming Venetian galleys (background). But most of his details—the armor, the cannons, the city walls—are from the 16th rather than the 13th century.

BIBLIOTHEQUE NATIONALE, SERVICE PHOTOGRAPHIQUE

The counter-weighted trebuchet was the easiest siege engine to build.

Before the expedition started, Doge Enrico had knelt weeping in the Church of St. Mark, and in the sight of all his people he donned a hat on which a cross had been sewn. When the fleet put out upon the waters, it seemed, said another crusader, Robert of Clari, "as if the whole sea swarmed with ants, and the ships burned on the water, and the water itself were aflame with the great joy that they had." They sailed across the Adriatic and camped before Zara. After an assault that lasted only five days, the city surrendered and was completely pillaged by the unrestrained Franks.

Despite protests from the Pope about the sack of a Christian city, the Crusade (if it could now be so called) prepared to go on. Montferrat joined the host at Zara, and with him came a firm proposal from young Alexius. If the crusaders would help him recover the throne of Byzantium, he would place the whole empire under the authority of Rome, thus uniting all of Christendom once again. Furthermore, he would give to the cause the enormous sum of 200,000 silver marks and would furnish 10,000 soldiers at his own expense. The barons discussed these attractive terms all through the winter at Zara, and the more they thought about them the more they liked them. A few objected, but there were many others who saw all the advantages in helping Alexius to the throne. Throughout every expedition to the East it had seemed to the Franks that the Byzantines were schemers and traitors. Now would be the time to force them to their knees. There were treasures beyond belief in Constantinople. And for the churchmen it seemed a heaven-sent chance to make the Eastern Church at last submit to Rome.

Young Alexius arrived in Zara in April, 1203. A few days later, those who remained with the Crusade put out to sea once more. They landed at the island of Corfu where they confirmed the treaty with Alexius and swore to help him. On June 24 they arrived before Constantinople. Says Villehardouin:

Now you may know that those who had never before seen Constantinople looked upon it very earnestly, for they never thought there could be in the world so rich a city; and they

The crusaders were not the last to see, and to covet, the rich beauty of Constantinople. In the 15th century, long after the Fourth Crusade, the city was taken by the Turks (right) who pitched their tents before the walls.

Le siège du grant turc auec ij defes principaulx conseilles

marked the high walls and strong towers that enclosed it . . . and the rich palaces and mighty churches . . . And be it known to you that no man there was of such hardihood but his flesh trembled; and it was no wonder, for never was so great an enterprise undertaken by any people since the creation of the world.

If the crusaders had been able to see the city of Constantinople from the air, it would have looked something like the head of a bull, with its great snout thrust out into the Bosporus and one huge, curling horn of an inlet on its head. That inlet from the Bosporus and the harbor all along the edge of the city were in fact called the Golden Horn, and on its other shore lay a separate quarter called Galata. The entrance to the Golden Horn was guarded by an enormous chain that stretched right across it. It lay just under the surface of the water and was fixed to a tower in Galata. Across the Bosporus on the Asiatic side lay two more suburbs, Chalchedon and Chrysopolis, really cities in their own right, which the crusaders first attacked, without success.

They landed then at Galata and launched their assault, hoping to capture the tower and release the chain so that their ships could sail into the harbor. After a fierce struggle, the attack succeeded. The crusaders broke the chain and the Venetians brought the siege engines and soldiers across the harbor and up to the walls of Constantinople itself. In the next two weeks they secured the whole harbor and then prepared for their land-and-sea assault on the city. Wrote Villehardouin:

They planted two ladders at a gate near the sea, and the wall was well defended by Englishmen and Danes [these were the famous Viking guards who served the emperor of Byzantium], and the attack was stiff and fierce. By main strength certain knights and two sergeants got up the ladders and made themselves masters of the wall; and at least fifteen got up on the wall and fought there, hand to hand, with axes and swords, and those within redoubled their efforts and cast them out . . . Meanwhile the Doge had not forgotten to do his part but had ranged his ships in line, and that line was three crossbow shots in length [perhaps five or six hundred yards] . . . Then might you have seen the mangonels shooting from the ships and transports, and the crossbow bolts flying, and the bows letting fly their arrows deftly and well; and those within defending the walls and towers very fiercely, and the ladders on the ships coming so near the walls that in many places swords and lances crossed; and the tumult and noise were so great that it seemed as if the very earth and sea were melting together.

Imperium Orientale. BY BAUDURI

LA VILLE ET LE PORT DE CONSTANTINOPLE

Le Bosphore de Trace

Canal de la Mer Noire

This was enough for the usurper, Emperor Alexius III. He packed up as much of his treasure as he could carry and left the city. The Greek soldiers of Byzantium took his blind brother, Isaac, from prison and set him upon the throne. Then they threw open the gates of the city so the crusaders could enter in triumph. Two weeks later young Alexius was crowned co-emperor with Isaac, who ratified the financial contract that had been made with the crusaders. It appeared that all obstacles had been cleared away. The crusaders could now go forth to fight the infidel, confident of a staunch ally in Byzantium.

But Alexius IV begged them to remain in Constantinople through the winter, for there was still a certain amount of opposition to him and it would be well for him to have these powerful supporters on hand until he was safely settled on the throne. Furthermore, the knights recognized that it would be dangerous and unnecessarily difficult to make a sea voyage during the winter months. So a fresh agreement was made: the crusaders would stay until March, 1204, and Alexius would pay all the expenses of the army and the fleet for a year.

No one knows, even today, whether all the decisions made by the chief barons of the Fourth Crusade, from the moment when the Crusade was diverted to Zara up to the events of this winter, were part of a careful and subtle plot or whether things just happened. But whatever the truth of the matter was, the purpose of the Crusade was then

Constantinople's defenders stretched a chain across the Golden Horn, an inlet of the Bosporus that divides the city from its suburb of Galata (upper right).

113

BURGERBIBLIOTHEK, BERN

bannarienfes

The crude painting above shows the mainstays of Venice's armed might: well-paid bowmen and ram-prowed ships using both sail and oars.

changed once and for all, the attack on Egypt forgotten.

To begin with, Alexius found it difficult to raise the money he had promised. There was constant conflict between the Greeks of the city and the westerners, so business came to a standstill. A terrible fire broke out—". . . the great churches and the rich palaces melting and falling in, and the great streets filled with merchandise burning." The city turned against its new emperor, and the Venetians did their best to stir up even more discord, arguing that it was time Constantinople had a Western emperor—one who would be ready, of course, to give Venice everything it wished for—and pointing out the riches that lay ready for the taking in the city.

Matters came to a head suddenly and violently. A number of Greek noblemen banded together under the

114

leadership of the first lord of the wardrobe, Murzuphlus, and in February they seized the palace. Young Alexius IV was strangled; Isaac died a few days afterward of illness, so it was said, but more likely of poison. Murzuphlus made himself emperor.

He did not last long. Open war between the Greeks and the crusaders broke out, and on April 12, 1204, the Western army stormed the city. Once again the ships landed troops on the shore and ladders were placed up against the walls. One tower was taken, then another. Gates were broken in; then the horses were taken from the transport ships and the knights mounted and rode into the city. Murzuphlus fled away, leaving his scarlet tents standing. That night, to prevent the Greeks from counterattacking, some of the Frankish soldiers set fire to another part of the city and once again hundreds of houses went up in flames. The next morning Montferrat rode along the shore and captured a stronghold by surprise; the rest of the host poured through the city, butchering the Greeks, looting, burning, until Constantinople was theirs.

They set aside three churches in which all the treasure was assembled. There it was divided: first between the Venetians and the Franks; then the crusaders paid out a further 50,000 marks of silver which were owed to the Venetians, and still, says Villehardouin, they had 100,000 marks left to divide among themselves. The division was, for those times, fair and equal. Two foot soldiers counted as one mounted man, and two mounted men counted as one knight. "No man received more, either on account of his rank or because of his deeds," wrote Villehardouin, "than that which had been so settled—except in so far as he may have stolen it."

One quarter of the plunder had been set aside to be given to the man the crusaders elected emperor. The Marquis of Montferrat, although he had been chosen chief of the Crusade in place of Count Thibaut, was not given the crown. Instead it went to Count Baldwin of Flanders. He had been one of the original leaders and had brought with him many men and more archers and crossbowmen than any other; in the attacks on the city he had led the vanguard. More important, as far as his election was concerned, was the fact that he was sponsored by the Venetians. Montferrat was given the kingdom of Thessalonica, in northeastern Greece, and the other nobles divided up the remaining European possessions of Byzantium among themselves, taking oaths of fealty to Emperor Baldwin.

UNIVERSITATSBIBLIOTHEK. HEIDELBERG

This soldier's mallet is about to discharge a trebuchet at a tower defended by an incautious bowman.

The exception, of course, was Venice. Three eighths of Constantinople was theirs, and they received a number of port cities and valuable Aegean islands, as well as the islands of Crete and Corfu.

But the various lords of this new empire had little time for the peaceful enjoyment of their possessions. They were immediately divided into bitter, quarreling factions. They were also attacked in increasing strength by the native population around them.

Fifty-seven years later the Latin Empire, as Frankish Byzantium was called, had collapsed. The descendants of Alexius III returned to Constantinople and recovered the city with the help of the merchant-soldiers of Genoa. The few advantages that had been gained by the Fourth Crusade vanished, as water vanishes on a hot stone.

The only benefits fell to the ambitious Italian businessmen. Their chief enemies were not the Saracens, but one another. Their fortunes rose and fell—sometimes Venice gaining power, sometimes Genoa or Pisa—but their own vast trading empire continued in the East for two hundred years after the end of the Latin Empire established by Count Baldwin and the Marquis of Montferrat. The Italians alone carried back home some of the wonderful treasures of Constantinople; it was their contact with the East which helped bring into being the revival in classical learning and art which we call the Renaissance. But their greed, which had helped to set on foot the Fourth Crusade, caused a rift between Eastern and Western Christianity that has endured to this day. And the Saracens, far from being weakened, became the masters of the East.

ITALIAN STATE TOURIST OFFICE

LOUVRE. PHOTO BY GIRAUDON

The romantic French painter Delacroix pictured the crusaders in the act of pillaging Constantinople.
Over St. Mark's portal are bronze horses (opposite) taken from the city in the Fourth Crusade.

117

VIII THE PERFECT KNIGHT

BIBLIOTHEQUE ST. GENEVIEVE, PARIS, PHOTO BY GIRAUDON

King Louis

In 1244 King Louis IX of France fell ill, and it was thought that he would die. He recovered, however, and in thanksgiving he vowed to take the cross. For once again word had come from the Holy Land that fresh forces were needed if the crusader states there were to survive. Yet, after three years of preparation, when King Louis at last set out, he did not go to the Holy Land after all because the direction of the Crusades was no longer toward Jerusalem. Echoing Montferrat and his ill-starred companions, the barons and princes now said that if you wish to kill a serpent you must cut off his head. The head of the Saracen serpent was Egypt.

An earlier crusading army had sailed in 1218 to capture the port of Damietta on the Nile. It was led by John of Brienne, King of Jerusalem, and with him were the Duke of Austria, the grand masters of the military orders, and a number of other nobles. They were accompanied by Cardinal Pelagius, the pope's legate. There was bitter fighting all through the winter, and the Moslems suffered as much from famine, weather, and internal disputes as the crusaders did. Furthermore, the Sultan al-Kamil faced downright treachery among his own people. At last he offered peace on excellent terms: if the Franks would leave Egypt he would return to them the True Cross, the city of Jerusalem, and all of central Palestine. Cardinal Pelagius refused to deal with the infidel, and he was supported by the masters of the Templars and the Hospitallers. Only a few days later the crusaders attacked Damietta, and this time they took the city.

They held it for two years. Then, on an unlucky expedition with a huge army up the Nile, they were cut off by the Sultan's ships. The Christians retreated in confusion

In midsummer, 1248, a knight named John of Joinville set out from his castle to go crusading with his lord, King Louis of France. As he glanced back at his home Sir John saw a scene much like this one of shearing and threshing that was painted for a devotional Book of Hours two hundred years later.

MUSÉE CONDÉ, CHANTILLY. PHOTO BY GIRAUDON

COURTESY OF PHILIP HOFER COLLECTION

Damietta, an Egyptian city at the mouth of the Nile River, was the first objective of the Sixth Crusade. King Louis, after voyaging to Cyprus (see map below), arrived before Damietta in 1249 and easily took the city. Main target of the Crusade was Cairo, since Egypt was then the center of Moslem power. After his defeat at Mansurah, Louis was ransomed off and went to rule in Acre where he had surprising success in his dealings with the Arabs.

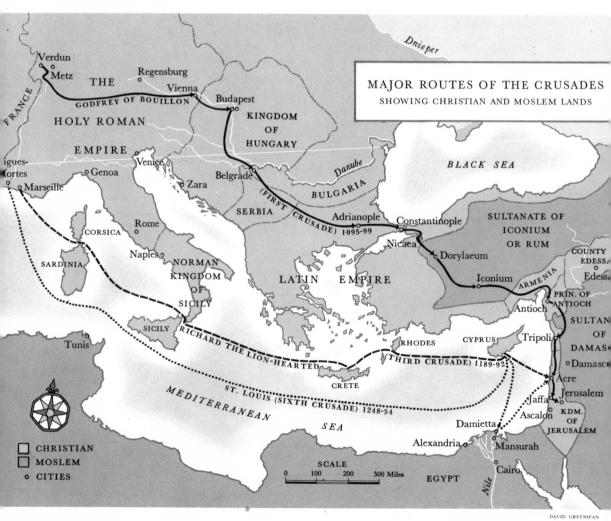

MAJOR ROUTES OF THE CRUSADES
SHOWING CHRISTIAN AND MOSLEM LANDS

Dnieper

Verdun
Metz
THE
Regensburg
Vienna
HOLY ROMAN
GODFREY OF BOUILLON
Budapest
KINGDOM
OF
HUNGARY
EMPIRE
FRANCE
igues-
ortes
Marseille
Genoa
Venice
Zara
Belgrade
Danube
BLACK SEA
Rome
SERBIA
BULGARIA
(FIRST CRUSADE)
1095-99
Adrianople
Constantinople
Nicaea
SULTANATE OF
ICONIUM
OR RUM
CORSICA
Naples
NORMAN
KINGDOM
OF
SICILY
LATIN EMPIRE
Dorylaeum
Iconium
ARMENIA
COUNTY
EDESSA
Edessa
SARDINIA
SICILY
RICHARD THE LION-HEARTED
RHODES
CYPRUS
Antioch
PRIN. OF
ANTIOCH
SULTAN
OF
DAMAS
Tripoli
Tunis
(THIRD CRUSADE) 1189-92
Damascus
Acre
Jerusalem
ST. LOUIS (SIXTH CRUSADE) 1248-54
CRETE
Jaffa
Ascalon
KDM.
OF
JERUSALEM
MEDITERRANEAN
SEA
Damietta
Alexandria
Mansurah
SCALE
0 100 200 300 Miles
Cairo
EGYPT
Nile

☐ CHRISTIAN
☐ MOSLEM
○ CITIES

DAVID GREENSPAN

MATTHEW PARIS *Chronicles*, CORPUS CHRISTI COLLEGE, CAMBRIDGE

Damietta was also the scene of the most bitter battle of the inglorious Fifth Crusade in 1218. A drawing of that battle (left) shows the great variety of headcoverings worn then: everything from mail hoods to steel caps and closed helms. It shows too the horrors of close-in fighting with swords and lances. At far left is the Damietta Charter, written after the capture of the city.

and thousands were killed in the mud and water. Pelagius, whether he liked it or not, had to deal with the Egyptians. He surrendered Damietta to al-Kamil and agreed to an eight-year truce.

The Fifth Crusade—which is how historians number the next attempt—was launched by Emperor Frederick II of Germany and the Holy Roman Empire. A man of great brilliance and very few morals, at first he refused to go to the East and was excommunicated by the pope. He laughed at excommunication; but in his own good time he went to Acre, arriving there in the fall of 1228.

For Frederick, religion was an interesting subject for study and argument, but that was about all. Cultured and intelligent, he began negotiating with the Moslems instead of fighting them, and after some four months of courteous bargaining without a blow being struck, he signed a treaty with al-Kamil. By its terms Jerusalem, along with several other cities and a narrow corridor to the sea, was returned to the Christians. All prisoners on both sides were freed, and a ten-year truce was to be observed.

Oddly enough, nobody liked this treaty. Moslems were enraged that so much had been given up, while Christians were equally furious that so little had been secured. When the truce ended, the country was plunged into war once again—chiefly between the Hospitallers and the Templars, who had now become so powerful and rich that they began fighting each other for control of various parts of the land. In 1244 the cavalry bands of the Khwarizmian Turks swept into Jerusalem. They left the city a ruin. This time the

Christians had lost the Holy City for good.

That was the news, then, which had come to France. But it did not prevent King Louis and his councillors from deciding to attack Egypt. Like the venturers of 1218, they too planned to take Damietta.

One of King Louis's chief councillors was the loyal knight John, the lord of Joinville, whose picturesque journal has been preserved. With great relish and an eye for detail, Sir John describes how he and his cousin sailed to the island of Cyprus where the King was gathering his troops, how various envoys arrived, and how supplies were gathered. He tells how King Louis took him into his service so that Joinville could pay his retinue, and he goes on to describe the departure of the host for Egypt in May, 1249. At dawn on June 4 they reached the coast before Damietta.

BIBLIOTECA VATICANA

The ships ran in to shore and Joinville was among the first to land. He and his men set their shields before them and planted the butts of their lances in the sand to make a hedge of spear-points. With drums beating and golden pennons flying, the galleys were run ashore and the knights leaped out and arrayed themselves beside the others. The Saracen army, with its gilded shields and banners, faced them. King Louis's banner, the *oriflamme* of St. Denis, was carried ashore, and the King himself sprang into the sea, which was up to his chest, and waded ashore to lead the assault. By evening the Saracens were in flight and people were leaving the city in panic. The next morning King Louis marched into Damietta in triumph.

The Nile began to rise, as it did every spring, flooding the land, and Louis decided to wait until the waters had receded again before marching on to Cairo, which the crusaders called "Babylon." Meanwhile, Sultan Ayub, the son of al-Kamil, offered to give up Jerusalem, as his father had before him, if the crusaders would leave Egypt. But Louis, as stubbornly intolerant as Cardinal Pelagius had been, would not bargain with the infidel. In October, reinforcements arrived from France, and the Frankish armies marched up the Nile until they reached the banks of a river opposite the strong city of Mansurah.

Emperor Frederick II

Apulia. BY C. A. WILKENSEN

The King ordered a causeway built across the river so that he could attack the Saracen camp. The workmen were protected by "cats," or sheds with covered towers. As fast as the Franks built up their earthen road, the Saracens dug away the banks on their side of the river so that the water could rush in, and thus nothing was gained. Joinville tells of the Greek fire that was hurled at the "cats"

TO BY GIRAUDON

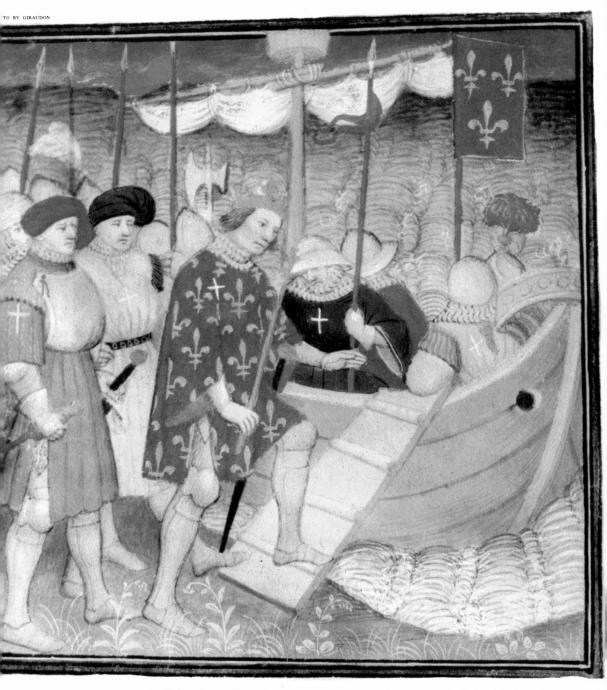

When the revered King Louis embarked on his Crusade (above), Christians knew that he would not compromise with the Moslems. Yet Emperor Frederick of the Holy Roman Empire, who preferred his books and his castles (left) to fighting, had accomplished more by one treaty than the valiant crusaders had gained by warfare.

123

and which struck such terror into the French that their only defense was to throw themselves on the ground in prayer.

The fashion of the Greek fire was such that it came frontwise as large as a barrel of cider, and the tail of fire that issued from it was as large as a long lance. The noise it made in coming was like heaven's thunder. . . . Every time that our saintly King Louis heard them hurling the Greek fire he would raise himself in his bed and say, weeping, 'Fair Lord God, guard my people!' And I believe that his prayers did us good service in our need.

After more than six weeks of battle, a native of the district offered to show the Franks a ford across the river if they would pay him five hundred gold pieces. The Templars were placed in the van; the second division was commanded by one of the King's brothers, the Count of Artois, a rash and headstrong man. On February 8, 1250, the army began to cross. In spite of the King's orders, Count Robert, who got his men over first, at once attacked the Egyptian camp. The Templars protested but had to follow him or be shamed. The attack was successful, but the Count, not content with overriding the enemy's tents, pushed on to the city of Mansurah with the Templars still behind him. There the Egyptians ambushed him, hurling beams and stones down upon the knights, who could not turn their horses in the narrow streets. Of the 290 Templars, only five got away; the Count of Artois and most of his followers were killed.

Meanwhile, the Christian army had been fighting up and down the river bank. We get a graphic picture of that battle from Joinville's account:

The Turks pressed upon me with their lances. My horse knelt under the weight and I fell forward over the horse's ears. I got up as soon as I could, with my shield at my neck and my sword in my hand . . . Everard of Siverey, who was one of my people, said that we should draw off to a ruined house and await the King . . . The Turks attacked us on all sides. . . . Hugh of Escot received three lance wounds in the face, and Frederic of Loupey received a lance wound between the shoulders, and the wound was so large that the blood flowed from him as from the bunghole of a cask. . . . Everard of Siverey said to me, 'Lord, if you think that neither I nor my heirs will be shamed by it, I will go and fetch help from the Count of Anjou.'

That help arrived, and Joinville, who had been wounded by a lance thrust and knocked over by a charge of Turkish horsemen, was rescued. He and his men returned to what he calls "a very fine passage of arms." He writes:

As I was there on foot with my knights . . . the King came up with his battalions . . . Never have I seen so fair a knight! For he towered head and shoulders above his people; and on his head was a gilded helm, and in his hand a sword of German steel.

. . . the Turks were driving back the King's other battalions, slashing and striking with swords and maces, and they forced back the other battalions upon the river . . . the stream was covered with shields . . . and with horses and men drowning.

Right straight upon us who were holding the bridge came Count Peter of Brittany, riding from Mansurah, and he had been wounded with a sword across the face, so that the blood ran into his mouth. . . . He had thrown the reins on the pommel of his saddle and held on with both hands so that his people who were behind him might not hustle him off the path . . . he spat the blood out of his mouth and said, 'Ha, by God's head, have you ever seen such riff-raff?'

We were all covered with the darts that failed to hit the sergeants. Now it chanced that I found a Saracen's quilted tunic . . . I opened it out and made a shield of it which did me good service, for I was only wounded by their darts in five places, and my horse in fifteen. . . . The good Count of Soissons, in that place of danger, jested with me and said, 'Seneschal, let these curs howl! By God's bonnet'—that was his favorite oath—'we shall talk of this day yet, you and I, in ladies' chambers.'

The King performed great feats of arms that day, once rescuing himself with hard sword strokes from six Turks who tried to catch his horse by the bridle. At last his troops drove the Egyptian army back, and he brought up his crossbowmen and sent them across the river on a hastily built bridge of boats. Under their fire the Egyptian resistance broke, and the field was left to the Franks. The King asked the provost of the Hospitallers if he had any news of Count Robert, his brother, and the provost said that the Count of Artois was in paradise. "But," said the provost, "be of good comfort, for never did king of France gain such honor as you have gained this day." The King replied, "Let God be worshiped for all He has given me." And then the big tears fell from his eyes for the sake of his dead brother.

The fighting was not yet over. That night there was an attack. Joinville and many of his people ran out wearing only quilted *gambesons* and steel caps, since because of the pain of their wounds they could not bear the weight of their armor. The Saracens were driven back, but three days later there was a hot and bloody battle when a reinforced Egyptian army attacked the French camp. Another of the King's brothers, Count Charles of Anjou, was hard

Like the horseman at right, knights of the later Crusades were more colorful than their predecessors. But warfare was no less deadly. Below are two skyline views of battle camps showing giant slings and catapults ready for firing, and in use.

ALL: BIBLIOTHEQUE NATIONALE, SERVICE PHOTOGRAPHIQUE

pressed, and Louis himself spurred to his help "with his sword in his fist, and dashed so far in among the Turks that they burnt the crupper of his horse with Greek fire." In the end, the Moslems were driven off with great losses.

But as matters turned out, these two victories were of little value. The Christian army sat where it was, for rumors had come that there was friction in the Egyptian ranks, and Louis hoped that the enemy might be weakened. Nothing of the sort happened—there was, it is true, trouble among members of the Egyptian court, but this did the Franks no good. The usual sicknesses of a military camp began to sweep through the Christian army— typhoid, scurvy, dysentery, and illness bred of the dampness, bad food, and lack of sanitation. The soldiers died by the hundreds. The Egyptians blockaded the river and cut off their supplies, and famine was added to the disease. After some eight weeks of this, it became clear to the King that he must retreat from the position.

For the sake of his men, he overcame his religious scruples and offered to exchange Damietta for Jerusalem. But this time the Sultan refused to deal with him, knowing that the French were in so bad a situation that he had only to wait for them to fall into his hands. The King's councillors urged him to go aboard a galley and escape, but he said proudly that he would never leave his people.

He himself had dysentery and could barely stand. The retreat began, and Louis, so ill that his attendants thought he was dying, was brought to a little village where he took shelter. Some of his barons sent a messenger to the Sultan to ask for a truce, but a treacherous sergeant rode through the ranks shouting that the King commanded them to surrender. Exhausted and tottering from illness, they laid down their arms. The Moslems moved in upon them and took the entire army prisoner. King Louis, who had given no such order, was chained and carried off to Mansurah.

There were so many prisoners that the Moslems, unable to feed or guard them all, simply killed the weakest or most badly wounded. The others were tormented and threatened, and at one point it seemed that the Egyptians were about to massacre them all. But in the end a treaty was arranged by which the King would give up Damietta and pay a ransom of half a million gold bezants before leaving the land, and a further half million when he had reached Acre.

All the money chests in the host were ransacked to find the ransom. The Templars at first refused to give any

MUSEO NAZIONALE, FLORENCE, PHOTO BY ALINARI

Even water vessels were made in the form of heroic knights.

PHOTO BY HOUVET

of their treasure, but Joinville, worn and thin and dressed in the ragged clothing of his imprisonment, went to their galley and by force took thirty thousand silver pieces. The character of the King may be measured by an incident that took place at Damietta during the counting of the money. Lord Philip of Nemours told Louis that they had saved him ten thousand silver livres by miscounting in their own favor. The King, instead of being pleased, was furious and said that he had given his word to pay the full amount. At this, Joinville nudged Lord Philip, who quickly said that he had only been joking. The King said gravely that such jests were not seemly. "I command you," he added, "by the fealty you owe me . . . that if these ten thousand livres have not been paid you will pay them without fail." Although his people urged him to go aboard a ship that was ready for sea, Louis would not stir until his promise had been carried out and the whole first payment of the ransom made.

Damietta was surrendered on May 6, 1250, and the crusaders sailed to Acre. There, in spite of letters from France urging him to return, the King decided to remain. The crusader states in the East had few men left after this failure, and the King felt he might strengthen them with whatever followers remained to him. In addition, he wished to wait until all the prisoners held by the Moslems had been released. Joinville, faithful as always, was one of those who stayed with him, although many of the other barons went back to France. He was given a battalion of fifty knights, and he became known for his courtesy, his

THE PIERPONT MORGAN LIBRARY

In a window of Chartres Cathedral in France, a young crusader knight is pictured receiving a red banner called the oriflamme. *It is this banner that King Louis is reported to have carried with him into battle. Louis (shown at right with his domineering mother, Queen Blanche) would have approved the zealous gleam in the young knight's eye, as well as the simple beauty of his dress.*

CORPUS CHRISTI COLLEGE, CAMBRIDGE

courage, and his large dinner parties.

For the next four years, Louis did his best to make the future of the Eastern kingdoms secure. He repaired the walls of many cities and tried to settle some of the unending quarrels between the barons. He searched for allies everywhere, among the Turks themselves and even among the far-off Mongols. But in France there was trouble brewing: the king of England threatened the land, and there were rumbles of civil war in the north. Still Louis might have remained longer in the Holy Land had it not been for the death of his mother.

Both Louis's mother, Queen Blanche of Castile, and his wife, Queen Margaret, were remarkable women. Until the time of her death, Queen Blanche had ruled France, as she had always ruled her son, with prim severity. Queen Margaret, who had been slighted consistently by her mother-in-law, had gone with Louis on his Crusade and had remained in Damietta where, only three days after the King was captured, she gave birth to a son.

The King set out for home on April 24, 1254, and the journey, like every sea voyage in those days, was full of peril. In spite of a nearly fatal shipwreck they came safely to land, and Joinville took leave of the King and Queen and journeyed home to his estates, which he had left so long before with such reluctance.

He had too much good sense to leave them again for the uncertain fortunes of a foreign land. When, in 1267, the King announced that he was taking the cross once more, Joinville not only refused to go with him but insisted that

Queen Margaret, like the agonized lady in the ship at right, had to cope with the peculiar perils and heartbreaks of the last Crusades. It was Margaret who nursed King Louis back to health before his departure for Egypt (above). And it was she who persuaded the Genoese seamen not to abandon her husband in Damietta. Finally, in 1270, she saw Louis and their son go to find death in the Seventh Crusade.

those who advised the King to go on this crusade were committing a mortal sin. "For at the point at which France then was, all the kingdom was at peace with itself and its neighbors," he wrote bitterly, "while ever since he [King Louis] departed, the state of the kingdom has done nothing but go from bad to worse." As for himself, Joinville said, while he was in the East his own lands had been ruined and his people had been beggared. "If I wished to do what was pleasing to God, I should remain here to help and defend my people, and if I put my body in danger in the pilgrimage of the cross, while seeing that this would be to the hurt and damage of my people, I should move God to anger."

He was, in the end, wiser than the King he so admired. For in 1270 Louis, already ill and tired, allowed himself to be persuaded to go, not to the Holy Land, but to Carthage,

BURGERBIBLIOTHEK, BERN

Discovery of the World, SIMON & SCHUSTER

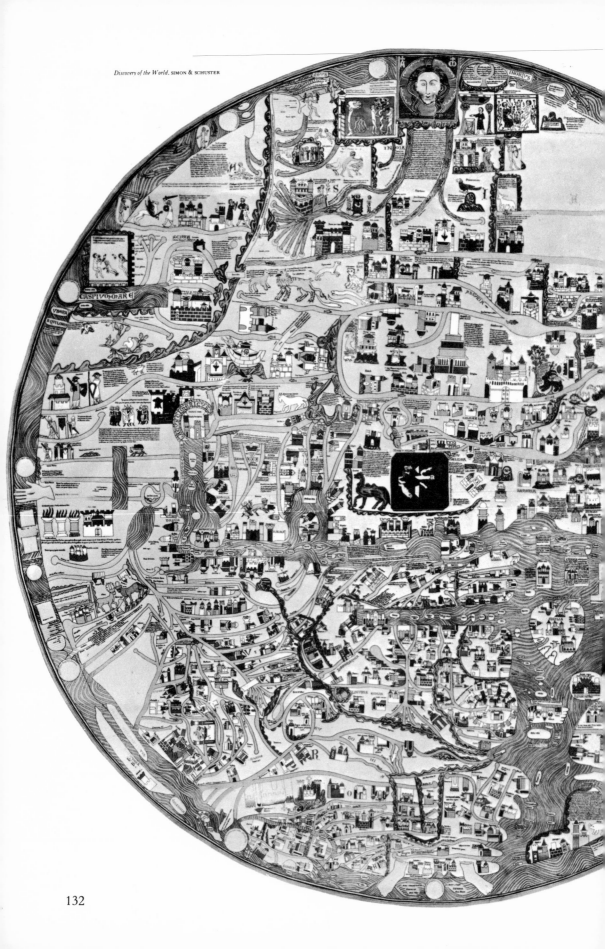

BIBLIOTHÈQUE NATIONALE

The later voyages of the sainted King Louis were complicated by the inadequate maps and crude navigational instruments of the Middle Ages. Most of the maps, like the famous Ebstorf world map at left, drew heavily from the realm of fantasy. Jerusalem is shown here as a large rectangle at the center of the earth. At right, an astronomer, a scribe, and a mathematician consult their instruments, many of which came to them from the Arabs.

in Africa, to bring Christianity to the ruler of Tunis. There disease spread through his camp, and he and his son —that young prince who had been born in Damietta—and half his army died of fever. "A piteous thing, and worthy of tears," wrote Joinville, "is the death of this saintly prince who kept and guarded his realm so holily and loyally."

Joinville lived on to the great age of ninety-three. In 1298 he had the satisfaction of seeing King Louis canonized by Rome, and he built an altar to Saint Louis in his own chapel in Joinville. When he was eighty-five he wrote his chronicle for the edification of Louis's grandson, the young prince who was to become King Louis X. Only four years before his death he answered the royal call to arms once more, and as old as he was, he rode out to war against the Flemings. He died in 1317, having spanned nearly the whole of the century that is often called "the golden age of knighthood."

Of all the crusaders, Saint Louis is perhaps the paragon. No one could ever claim he looked for personal gain; he was upright and just, both as a king and as a man, and he put his religion into daily practice as no ordinary person could. It might have been far better for his own land and for the Latin kingdoms in the East if he had never taken the cross, for thousands of lives were lost and nothing was gained. Worse, there was a spiritual loss which could not be repaired. Churchmen had argued in the past that the Crusades had ended in disaster because of the sins of their leaders. But if a man as saintly as Louis could not win back the Holy Land, then perhaps these ventures were not pleasing to God at all. The death of King Louis marks the point at which the heart of the crusading movement failed. The age of the great Crusades was over.

وَكَادَ يَنْزِعُ الجِمَالَ الشُّمُسَ وَأَنْشَدَ

مَا الحَجُّ سَيْرُكَ تَأْوِيبًا وَإِدْلَاجًا وَلَا غَنَاءَكَ أَجْمَالًا وَأَحْدَاجًا

الحَجُّ أَنْ تَقْصِدَ البَيْتَ الحَرَامَ عَلَى تَحْرِيكِكَ الحَجَّ لَا تَبْغِي بِهِ حَاجًا

وَتَمْضِيَ كَابِلِ الإِنْصَافِ مُتَّخِذًا رَدْعَ الهَوَى هَادِيًا وَالحَقَّ مِنْهَاجًا

IX THE KNIGHTS' TWILIGHT

One of the fiercest of Saint Louis's foes had been a Turkish prince named Baibars, who was called the Crossbowman. It was he who had rallied the Egyptians in Mansurah, trapping and slaughtering the Templars and the men of Count Robert of Artois in the narrow streets. Coming to Syria as a slave, Baibars had been chosen for the sultan's palace guard, the famed Mamelukes, and he had swiftly risen to a position of great importance. Gigantic, energetic and intelligent, but utterly without mercy, he gathered power until, in the year 1260, he murdered the ruling sultan and was able to make himself the lord of Egypt. He united the East, as Saladin had, and he was like Saladin in his determination to sweep the Christians from Syria and the Holy Land.

As usual, his enemies were divided. Venice and Genoa still struggled for commercial supremacy; the Templars and Hospitallers, swollen with wealth, looked to their own interests; the barons could not agree on a leader. Baibars stormed town after town, and when his Christian foes surrendered to him on promise of their lives, he did not hesitate to break his word; those who were not sold as slaves were beheaded. One of his castles was completely surrounded by the heads of prisoners, impaled on stakes.

In 1268, Antioch fell to him. The city which had been the first of the Frankish holdings and which had been taken by Bohemond's cunning in the First Crusade was plundered and ruined. All but a handful of its inhabitants were either killed or enslaved.

During the next nine years, Baibars swept across the land. When he died of poison in 1277, the Christian pos-

METROPOLITAN MUSEUM OF ART, GIFT OF JUNIUS S. MORGAN

Arab caravans like the one being whipped and trumpeted along at the left came into the crusader states from the East. When Prince Edward of England (at right) arrived in the Holy Land, he was shocked to note the commercial atmosphere and the trade being carried on between Christians and Moslems.

135

ARAB INFORMATION CENTER

One of the last crusader castles to fall was Markab in Syria.

sessions had shrunk to no more than half a dozen coastal cities. Twelve years later, Tripoli was taken by the Egyptians; and two years after this disaster, Acre, the greatest of the Frankish fortress-cities, was captured. The end of the century saw the end, at last, of the Western kingdoms in the East. All that had been won in the Holy Land by the long series of holy wars was lost, finally and forever.

There had been some attempts to send reinforcements from Europe to fight against Baibars, but the crusading spirit was fading. King James I of Aragon sailed out in 1269, but his ships were turned back by a storm. His two sons went to Acre with a small army, but they accomplished nothing and soon went home again.

The last crusader who might have done anything to stop Baibars was a man destined to play a large role in the later development of Europe. That was Prince Edward of England, an able, vigorous, but cold-blooded knight to whom early quests such as the rescue of the True Cross seemed rather pointless.

After journeying to the Holy Land and landing at Acre in 1271, Edward realized that the armed forces at his command were far too small to challenge Baibars successfully. With all his diplomatic skill he tried to get the comfortable barons of the crusader states to join with him, but they failed to see the nearness of their doom and refused their support. They were lulled into a false understanding of the security of their position by the belief that there would always be crusaders coming to their defense and by the continued promises of assistance from the eastern Mongols, who were Baibars' greatest enemy.

Edward had a better understanding of the times than the barons, although even he must have wondered about the mysterious disappearance of the crusading spirit. He concluded that it would be useless to assault the Egyptians again, and he returned to England in 1272. His return coincided with the death of his father, and he became King Edward I of England—one of the last knights of the Crusades and one of the first modern monarchs of Europe.

When compared with great sweeping changes in world history, the Crusades seem more of an adventurous fiasco than a significant episode. But men and nations cannot endure an experience as intense as the Crusades without

The beginning of the end of the crusader states was the fall of Tripoli to the sultan of Egypt in 1289. The walled seaport, already weakened by trade rivalries, was doomed when the Venetian and Genoese fleets deserted.

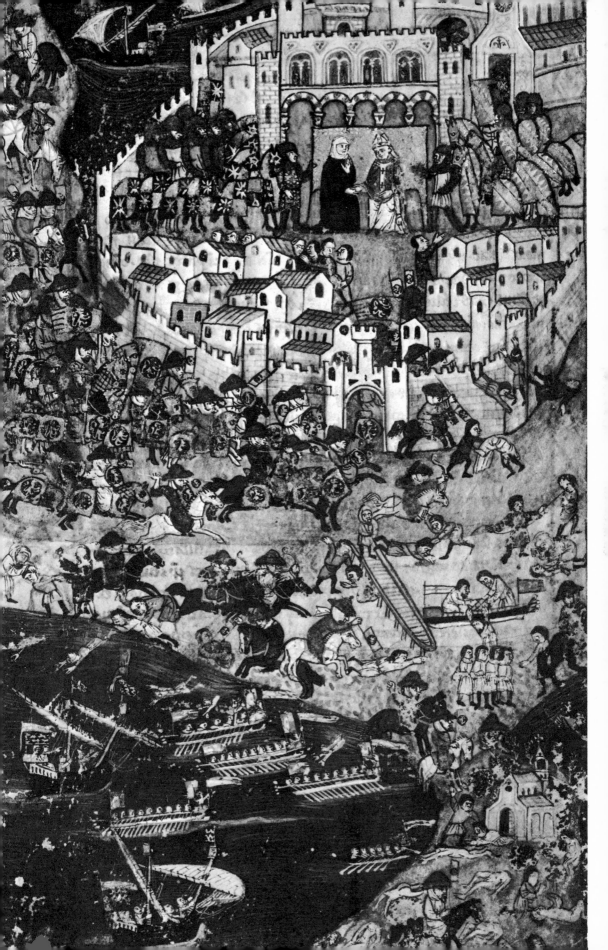

From Rome, and from monasteries such as Italy's
Monte Cassino (above), the Church struggled to
maintain its leading position in Europe. At times
this involved the use of armed might to settle
theological disputes. The so-called Albigensian
Crusade, in which the French city of Carcassonne
(right) was stormed in 1209, was nothing more
than a suicidal debate among fellow Christians.

being deeply affected by it. And, as the crusading era ended, a question arose: How would the knights who emerged from the Crusades fare in Europe? Would they sweep all before them and come to rule their native lands with wisdom?

The knight returned to Europe with high expectations. He had learned new ways of fighting, he had seen distant lands and dazzling courts of fabulous wealth, and he was not about to settle for the old life in his isolated and cheerless rural manor. He was a chivalric figure, and chivalry had come to include the idea of living well—as would befit a member of a noble order. To be a knight now meant largess, the giving of alms, and the necessary wealth to maintain servants and men-at-arms. It meant the expense of a fine castle and lands, feasts and fine equipment, comfort and beauty.

What astonished the knight the most about the new face of Europe, however, was not his fellow nobles' more abundant way of life; it was that there were so many other people who expected to live well. Farms and fields in Europe had spread and the wild forests were shrinking. The countryside was dotted with cities and towns in which

The Children's Crusade, an embarrassment to the Church, began in 1212 when a French boy, preaching in the manner of Peter the Hermit, led several thousand of his young followers to Marseilles (right) where they expected the waters to open so they could walk to the Holy Land. Many of them fell instead into the hands of merchants who sold them to slave dealers.

GUSTAVE DORE

FRENCH GOVERNMENT TOURIST OFFICE

139

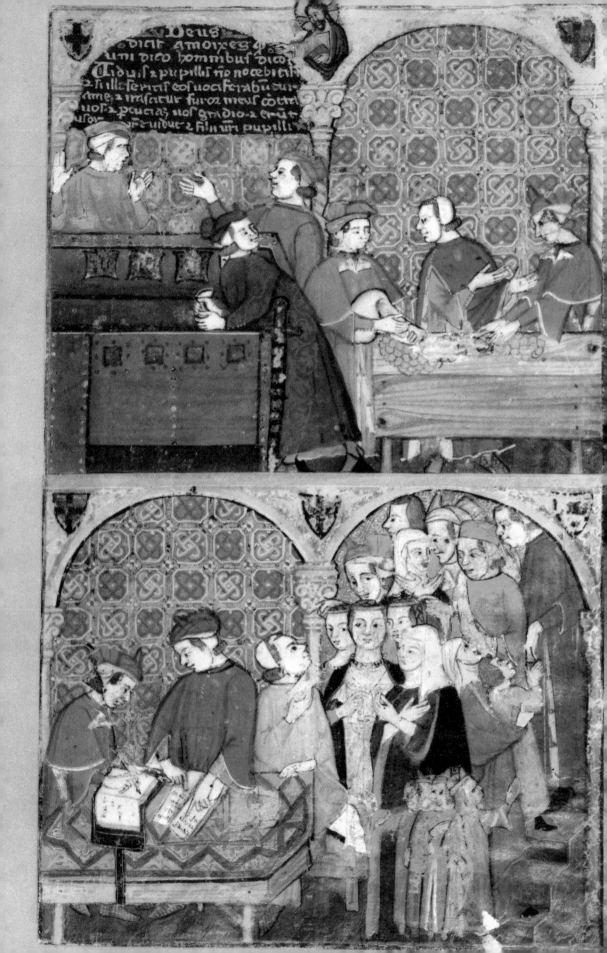

Deus
dirit a moixeg q̃
uni diro hommibus dico
Eiduis z pupilli no nocebitis
z illi serierit eos uocaferabūdur
ame z irasitur furoz meus cōtra
uos z peuciaz uos gradio z erūt
uxors forerilidur z filii ūi pupilli

busy merchants, bankers, and artisans carried on their work and found themselves growing rich.

In 1100 what might have been a small town with a few artisans working at handicrafts and a few small merchants doing a little buying and selling at markets had burst out of its walls by 1300 and become a wealthy, bustling center of trade.

Indeed, the two centuries of the Crusades accelerated the whole process of wider trade and growing cities that characterized the later Middle Ages. It was inevitable that there should be rivalry and bitter clashes between the nobility of the land and the new aristocracy of the cities. Everywhere, the divisions within society were sharpening. The next two centuries would see growing unrest, uprisings of peasants and of working people in the towns, pressure for more rights, privileges, and liberties. Already, the power of kings had grown. They were no longer merely the lords of little states; their countries were becoming nations, slowly but surely, and the awful majesty of the crown was increasing.

But, for the moment, Europe was still controlled by the might of the mailed horseman. Knighthood, which had won the day at Senlac and had gone on to battle in the Crusades, was still the greatest force in the medieval world. Yet the turning of the century, the last years of the thirteenth and the early years of the fourteenth centuries, saw two vital incidents, both of them battles, which foreshadowed what was to come. It is unlikely that those who took part in them, men like England's King Edward, fully understood their meaning. And yet each battle, in its way,

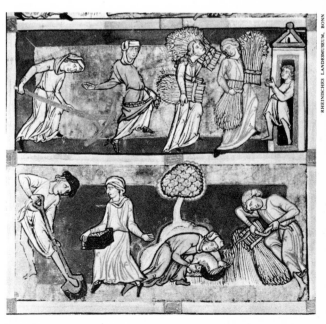

RHEINISCHES LANDESMUSEUM, BONN

The richness of a new age was spread across Europe. Now it was not only the knight who lavishly decorated his home and who expected to be treated as an aristocrat but wealthy merchants and bankers as well. The luxurious offices of the Genoese banker (left), with their tiled walls and vaulted ceilings, were elegant enough to admit high-born ladies. Even the peasants (right) were finding prosperity by leaving the land for the freedom of the cities.

was to alter the course of history as decisively as the Battle of Hastings in 1066.

The first of these battles took place near Falkirk in Scotland. King Edward I had been king of England for twenty-six years. His men called him "Longshanks"; a tall, handsome man, typically one of the Plantagenets, with fair hair, great strength, and a liking for rough sports, hunting, the tourney, and war. His land was no longer Norman and Saxon; it was becoming English and had even begun to think of itself in national terms rather than as a collection of small baronies and earldoms. The larger task now fell to Edward of drawing under his rule the stubbornly rebellious Welsh on the western border and the Scots of the north. Scotland had risen against him in the year 1297, and the following year Edward marched with his army to fight William Wallace, the leader of the rebels.

As at Senlac, the Scots placed themselves in a defensive position on a hillside near the edge of a vast forest. They were in four large divisions of perhaps five thousand men each, all on foot and all armed with the broad-bladed Scottish pike, a heavy spear with a shaft twelve feet long. Behind the footmen were a thousand horsemen, and supporting them were a few thousand archers. They stood fast, sure that any cavalry charge would not be able to get through their solid ranks.

Edward had three thousand mailed knights and four thousand other mounted men-at-arms, as well as some eight or nine thousand foot soldiers, most of whom were Welsh or English archers. It was apparent from the English knights' first charge that the Scottish spearmen, kneeling side by side, would not give way. But then King Edward used a tactic he had heard of in the Crusades and had learned to respect in his wars against the Welsh. He brought forward his archers and ordered them to shoot at certain points in the Scottish front. The long arrows whistled through the air and dropped in a deadly shower upon the pikemen, who dared not move out of their ranks. They fell by the hundreds. Only a few minutes of this awful sleet was enough. Now the English knights could ride forward and strike at those places where the arrows had done their worst work, where there were large gaps in the Scottish lines. They burst through. The pikes were too long for close work, and the divisions were scattered. A full third of the Scots were slain, and the rest fled into the forest.

The important difference between this engagement and

Famous Harlech Castle was b[ui]
by King Edward after his ret[urn]
from the Crusades. It domina[tes]
a Welsh valley, just as the c[ru]
sader castles defended Palesti[ne]

many others like it lay in the battle plan—and in the bows —that Edward's archers used. They were neither the short-bows the Normans had used at Senlac nor the crossbows so favored by Richard the Lion-Heart and the crusading knights who came after him. They were a new weapon— new, at any rate, to Europe. They were six-foot long-bows. A man could shoot half a dozen arrows with one of these bows while a crossbowman was preparing to loose his second bolt.

King Edward understood their value and was to use them often. But for him, and for later kings, they were no more than auxiliary weapons, useful as a support for cavalry but hardly more than that. War—real war—still rested upon the clash of armored knights, and after Falkirk, all that noblemen remembered was the final charge of cavalry. The longbow, however, was more than just another weap-

143

on. It was one of the things that kept the English yeoman a free man, unlike the poorly armed peasantry of many other lands. In the course of the next two centuries, it was to prove decisively that a man on foot could bring down the most heavily armored horseman. It was to make the ordinary foot soldier the equal, and finally the master, of the chivalry of Europe. There must have been many English and Welsh farmers who never forgot that it was really the longbow that had beaten the Scots at Falkirk.

The second sign of the knight's decline occurred four years afterward, many miles from Falkirk, and under quite different circumstances.

The towns of Flanders—what is today Belgium and part of Holland—were the main producers of woolen cloth. The masters of the weavers' guilds and the merchants who bought wool and sold cloth were rich men, richer and prouder than many a knight or baron. The mass of the townsfolk were sturdy and independent, ready to fight for their rights against their own town governments or against any outsider who threatened them.

The Count of Flanders, Guy of Dampierre, was the vassal of the French king; but he wished to be on the best terms possible with England, for it was from England that the wool came for the looms of Flanders. He made an alliance with King Edward I and planned a marriage between his daughter and the King's son. This was a violation of his oath of fealty, and his overlord, King Philip the Fair of France, had him clapped into prison. French troops marched into Flanders to hold the land directly for Philip.

The Flemish towns buzzed like a nest of hornets. There were riots against the French men-at-arms and the French governor, and at last the burghers rebelled outright. The French garrison in Bruges was destroyed. Everywhere, the townspeople rallied together until they had formed a large army.

Against them, King Philip sent the pick of the chivalry of France. Hundreds of glittering knights and noblemen and thousands of men-at-arms, led by Count Robert of Artois, the grandson of that same rash crusading Count Robert who had been killed at Mansurah, went to subdue the burghers. They met the Flemings, who were clothed in somber woolens and armed only with pikes and bows, before the walls of the city of Courtrai on July 11, 1302.

A shallow stream lay between the two armies, and the burghers had a river on their left, a marsh on their right,

WOODCUT AFTER MINIATURE IN BRITISH MUSEUM

Steadying his clumsy weapon with his left foot, this archer is cocking a crossbow by means of a winch that draws the string to its notch.

144

and behind them was the city. Studying the ground, Count Robert decided he had them in a trap. He would hurl them back against the city walls, ride them down, and then at his leisure kill those who floundered away in the marsh or the river. His trumpets sounded and the first rank of knights lowered their lances or drew their swords and trotted forward.

They splashed through the stream and began pressing up the slope on top of which the Flemings stood. The steep hill, the heat, and the weight of their arms slowed them, so that some dropped back and their lines became ragged. The burghers, instead of fleeing, lowered their pikes and ran to meet them in one solid mass.

It was a slaughter—but of the other side. Horses went down, plunging and screaming, and the knights were pinned under them. They could not reach their enemies with sword or lance; the long-handled pikes swept them from their saddles. They were hampered by their mail, their shields, and their helmets, or tangled in their surcoats and the trappings of their horses; before they could struggle to their feet, the townsmen leaped on them and slew them without mercy.

Count Robert himself led the charge of his second line. They had even more trouble than the first, for now they had to pick their way over fallen men and kicking horses. The marsh and the river were a trap indeed; not for the burghers, but for the knights who could not ride round to fall on the Flemish flanks but had to come straight at them. Once more the pikemen rolled forward, and once again the proud line of knights went down. The Count was killed; the rest of the French, including the infantry, which had not even come near the battle, did not try to face those awful spears. They ran, as they had expected to see the Flemish towns-people run.

Seven hundred pairs of golden spurs were hacked from the heels of dead knights and hung up as trophies in the church of the Abbey of Groeningen in Courtrai. It was not to be believed that the gallant knights of France had been routed by fat burghers, common weavers and cloth makers, base villains who worked for their living. But the seven hundred pairs of spurs glittered in the candlelight of the church as proof that it had happened.

Within a few short years knights were to have their revenge at Mons-en-Pevele and Cassel, where they smashed armies of burghers. They could then tell themselves that it was not the pikes but the marsh and rivers which had

N.Y. PUBLIC LIBRARY

First used by the Welsh, the longbow had advantages over the crossbow: it was more accurate, and faster on the draw.

145

MUSÉE CONDÉ, CHANTILLY. PHOTO BY GIRAUDON

In the 14th century knights had the time and the means to become lords of Europe. And when they rode out on a procession with their ladies, accompanied by pages and pets (left), they presented a colorful scene indeed. But they found that other forces contested their exclusive right to the good things of life. The Flemish townspeople at right, wearing plate armor, are shown fighting richly equipped French knights at the Battle of Courtrai. Fought near Ghent, Belgium, in 1302, this so-called Battle of the Golden Spurs was won by the daring Flemish citizens, and their victory proved that the era of the knights was drawing to a close.

beaten them at Courtrai. They could boast that defeat was the proper fate of any insolent commoner, any foot soldier who tried to stand up to a cavalry charge. But the knightly power so firmly established at Senlac and proven in the Crusades was already threatened. The long-bow, drawn by hard-handed yeomen who prided themselves on their freedom, was to bring the knighthood of Europe crashing to the ground. And the cities, growing, building, spreading, were to put an end to feudalism itself, to beggar the knights, and finally to absorb their lands, their titles, and their rank.

The age of chivalry had another two lingering centuries of life before it ended. Even though the order of knighthood was to pass, it would leave behind it a shining residue, like gold dust in a pan. The ideal of the "gentle, perfect knight" was achieved by very few men. But as an ideal it affected many lives, and no one can help being stirred by the virtues of chivalry: to be loyal, to be humble, to serve man and God, to be courageous in the face of all odds, and to be courteous. Chaucer's Knight loved "truth and honor, freedom and courtesy." Out of the bloody violence of knighthood, these rose as high and worthy goals for any man in any future generation.

OVERLEAF: *Courtrai Castle, shown at lower left in this wood carving, was the scene of the climax of the battle. To avoid being killed by the victorious townspeople, one of the knights escapes from a tower.*
NEW COLLEGE, OXFORD

147

COLLECTION OF LT. COL. J. WEST OF SAWTRY, ENG.

A portrait of the 14th-century knight Sir Geoffrey Luttrell is one of the crusading era's most beautiful illuminations. It shows him getting ready for knightly combat with the aid of not one but two ladies.

AMERICAN HERITAGE PUBLISHING CO., INC.

BOOK DIVISION

RICHARD M. KETCHUM, *Editor*

HORIZON CARAVEL BOOKS

RUSSELL BOURNE, *Editor*

MERVYN D. KAUFMAN, *Assistant Editor*

JUDITH HARKISON, *Chief Picture Researcher*

LUCY DAVIDSON, *Picture Researcher*

EVELYN H. REGISTER, *Picture Researcher*

ELAINE K. ANDREWS, *Copy Editor*

JANET CZARNETZKI, *Art Director*

GERTRUDIS FELIU, *European Bureau*

ACKNOWLEDGMENTS

The Editors are deeply indebted to the curators of several rare book libraries in which manuscript illuminations of special value to this book were found. Foremost among them are Miss Mary Kenway and Mr. John Baglow of The Pierpont Morgan Library in New York City; M. Jean Porcher, Chief Curator of the Manuscript Department in the Bibliothèque Nationale, Paris; Dr. Christophe Von Steiger, Manuscripts Curator in the Burgerbibliothek, Bern, Switzerland; and the staff of the Manuscript Department in the British Museum. Special thanks are also owed to Sir Steven Runciman, author of the authoritative *A History of the Crusades*, who gave generously of his time in reading the narrative; and to Major L. C. Gates, Honourable Secretary of the Battle Historical Society, Battle, England. In addition, the Editors wish to thank the following individuals and organizations for their assistance and for making available material in their collections:

Padre Gregorio Andres Martinez Agustino, Director of the Biblioteca del Monasterio de El Escorial, Madrid, Spain

Mrs. Judy Koch, Israel Government Tourist Office, New York

Mr. Joseph L. Graham, American Historical Company, Inc., New York

Mr. George Wehr, Coin Galleries, Inc., New York

Miss Dorothy Miner, Librarian and Keeper of Manuscripts, The Walters Art Gallery, Baltimore

Don Ireneo Daniele, Seminario di Padova, Padova, Italy

Prof. Dr. C. Wehmer, Director, Universitätsbibliothek, Heidelberg, Germany

Padre Leccisotti, Bibliotecario del Monastero di Monte Cassino, Italy

M. Paul Eeckhout and M. Max Servais, Musée des Beaux Arts, Ghent, Belgium

Mr. Robert W. Hill and Mr. Anthony Cardillo, New York Public Library

Graf Von Spee, Castle Heltorf, Germany

Special research and photography; New York—Arnold Eagle, Geoffrey Clements; England—Timothy Green; Scotland—Zoltan Wegner; Italy—Maria Todorow; Spain—John Mosly

FURTHER REFERENCE

Readers interested in further examining the arts and armaments of the crusading era may find exhibits of varying kinds in many American cities. Two of the most pertinent exhibits are the reconstructed medieval monasteries in New York City (The Cloisters) and The Old Spanish Monastery in North Miami Beach. Other exhibits that also are open to the public may be found in the following cities: Baltimore—The Walters Art Gallery; Boston—Museum of Fine Arts; Chicago—Art Institute of Chicago; Cleveland—The Cleveland Museum of Art; Denver—Denver Art Museum; Detroit—Detroit Institute of Arts; New York—The Metropolitan Museum of Art and The Pierpont Morgan Library Exhibition Hall; Philadelphia—Museum of Art; Seattle—Seattle Art Museum; Washington, D.C.—The Dumbarton Oaks Collection of Byzantine Art.

For those who wish to read more about the Crusades, the following books are recommended:

Adams, Henry. *Mont-Saint-Michel and Chartres*. New York: Doubleday, 1959.

Ambroise. *The Crusade of Richard Lion-Heart*. Translated by Merton J. Hubert. New York: Columbia University Press, 1941.

Ashdown, Charles H. *Armour & Weapons in the Middle Ages*. London: G. G. Harrap, 1925.

Coe, Frederick. *Knight of the Cross*. New York: Sloane, 1951.

Coulton, G. G. *The Medieval Scene*. England: Cambridge University Press, 1959.

Cripps-Day, Francis Henry. *The History of the Tournament in England and in France*. London: B. Quaritch, Ltd., 1918.

Doyle, Sir Arthur Conan. *The White Company*. New York: McKay, 1961.

Duggan, Alfred L. *Knight with Armour*. London: Faber and Faber, 1950.

Evans, Joan. *Life in Medieval France*. London: Phaidon Press, 1957.

Fedden, Robin. *Crusader Castles*. Chester Springs, Pa.: Dufour, 1957.

Hitti, Philip K. *History of the Arabs*. New York: St. Martin's Press, 1960.

Huizinga, Johan. *The Waning of the Middle Ages*. New York: Doubleday, 1954.

Kelman, Janet Harvey. *Stories from the Crusades*. New York: E. P. Dutton, 1907.

Lamb, Harold. *The Crusades*. Doubleday, 1945.

Meller, Walter C. *A Knight's Life in the Days of Chivalry*. New York: Greenberg, Inc., 1924.

Muntz, Hope. *The Golden Warrior*. New York: Scribner's, 1949.

Oldenbourg, Zoé. *The Cornerstone*. Translated by Edward Hyams. London: V. Gollancz, 1954.

Oman, Sir Charles W. C. *A History of the Art of War in the Middle Ages*. New York: B. Franklin, 1959.

Pernoud, Regine. *In the Steps of the Crusaders*. New York: Hastings, 1960.

Pyle, Howard. *Men of Iron*. New York: Globe, 1954.

Runciman, Steven. *A History of the Crusades*. England: Cambridge University Press, 1952-54.

Scott, Sir Walter. *Ivanhoe*. New York: Doubleday, 1943.

Villehardouin, Geoffrey de. *Memoirs of the Crusades*. Translated by Sir Frank T. Marzials. New York: E. P. Dutton, 1958.

Williams, Jay. *The Siege*. New York: Little, Brown, 1954.

INDEX

Bold face indicates pages on which maps or illustrations appear

153